TALES OF
THE
MINE COUNTRY

Eric McKeever

The Old Colliery, Shamokin, Pennsylvania

Dedication

To Florence, the miner's daughter that I married, and to all miners, past, present and future, with the greatest respect.

Abandoned breaker near Gilberton, Pennsylvania.

Library of Congress Catalog Card Number: 94-184891
ISBN: 0-9643905-0-7

Table of Contents

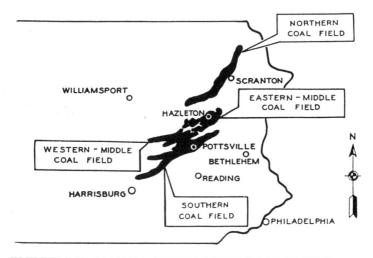

THE PENNSYLVANIA ANTHRACITE COAL FIELDS

This map is used by permission of the Applied Arts Publishers, Box 479, Lebanon, PA 17042. It is from the splendid publication, "When Coal Was King," by Louis Poliniak, recounting the history, in many photographs, of the early coal mining period.

The coal beds were vast, stretching for miles. Near Pottsville, the Mammoth Vein was 70 feet thick. The wealth of the coal fields gave rise to the Reading Coal and Iron Company and the Reading Railroad. Together, they were the largest commercial enterprise in the United States, about a century ago. Coal provided the energy for the development of the railroad and steel industries of this nation.

INTRODUCTION

This is a collection of memories of a time and place. The time was in my childhood during the 1930's, the place was Shamokin, Pennsylvania, a small coal mining town in the north-eastern part of the state. Some of the tales are true, some may be only partly so. Most of the principals involved are long dead, with no way to verify the accuracy of what was related.

The stories set forth here are not meant to be necessarily factually accurate, nor yet again any sort of documentary of the mines, people, or history of the area. Information received in childhood may be true, partly true, or not at all true. The event of the dinky cable rolls is certainly true, in that I was one of the boys who rolled them down the culm bank. As to whether the Cameron mine was precisely 2000 feet deep, or 7 miles to the workface, I do not have specific knowledge.

In these tales I am attempting to convey a feel for the lives of people who lived by mining. There was a movie made entitled "The Molly Maguires" that was singularly dreary, boring, monotonous, and dispiriting. It was probably a fairly good representation of the lives of the miners in the late 1800's.

My wife's father was a mine laborer. He was an infantryman in the First World War and was gassed in combat. He subsequently developed black lung (anthrasilicosis) from mining, and emphysema from heavy smoking. Mike was a gentlemanly fellow. He didn't expect much out of life, and he didn't get very much either, but he didn't complain. He was nearing the end of his life when I met him. Shortly after my wife and I were married, he was taken to the Veteran's Hospital at Wilkes-Barre with pneumonia, which was common among miners. He was placed in an oxygen tent, while some family members anxiously gathered around, and asked if they could do anything for him.

"Yeah, get me outta here," he responded.

"They're trying to save your life, Mike," said his wife.

"They ain't gonna save my life. I want to die at home. Take me home so I can smoke a couple more cigarettes. I get lonesome for them."

The relatives did take him home, he did smoke a few more cigarettes, whereupon he lapsed into a coma and was returned to the hospital, where he died. These stories are a small tribute to Mike, to Grandpa Bert and Grandpa Eddie, to Great Grandpa John (the Molly Maguire), and to the thousands of other men in the mines who lived out their lives in brutal toil, deadly danger, and certain debility if they survived.

The Molly Maguires originated in Mahanoy City in the middle 1800's. They were a vigilante group who employed terror and violence to intimidate mine owners for their cruelly repressive working conditions. My great grandfather and his brothers were Molly Maguires in Mahanoy City. This knowledge impelled me to make an informal research effort about a year ago. I have concluded that they were not the idealistic social reformers that some of the descendants might wish to think, but that there was much merit in their struggle against incredibly poor and dangerous working conditions. This conflict, with the loss of dozens of lives on each side, marked the beginning of the labor movement in the United States.

In the mining towns, if you arose and went outdoors early of a summer morning, as you walked by the little wooden row houses, you would hear the miners in the morning ritual of coughing, great racking, gasping coughs, which lasted 10 or 20 minutes. This sound was as natural as the birds singing in the trees. If you became a miner, you knew that you would do "bull work," and when you reached old age (anything past 50), you would gasp and wheeze, and spit up in the coal bucket by the coal stove. This was the life of the miner.

The Mahanoy Creek at Girardville. There are many pretty woodland scenes in the coal region.

Photo by Christine Goldbeck of the *Shenandoah Evening Herald.*

Uncle George

Uncle George was a very handsome man when he was young. The young women took note of this, and made it plain to him that they did. This was in the 1920's, and he would go to the Lithuanian Club and dance the Lithuanian dances, drink beer, make jokes, and altogether enjoy himself. He worked in the mine at Port Griffith, close by the Susquehanna River near Wilkes-Barre and Scranton, in the hard coal region of Pennsylvania.

The mine was probably no more or less dangerous than most others of the time and place. One day the roof fell in. A large flat rock smashed Uncle George's face, with other rocks doing damage to him. The rock fall was not very serious, so the other miners dug him out, put him on the hood of a car, and carried him to a local hospital. Plastic surgery was not much known in those days, and even if it had been, no one was much interested in salvaging the face of a poor immigrant Lithuanian mine laborer.

Uncle George was my wife's uncle. When we were first married, we'd go to stay at the home of Aunt Pauline in Wyoming, Pennsylvania. Aunt Pauline was Uncle George's sister. Uncle George was a curious figure, silently shuffling around the house, never looking at us or acknowledging a greeting. He would mutter a few words to Aunt Pauline, and quickly leave. He was in his sixties then, and from the time of the accident had spoken to almost no one except Aunt Pauline.

He never returned to the mine, but worked as a handy man and janitor at a nearby saloon, bothering no one, keeping to himself, and being strange in his own quiet way. He was not rude when he did not speak to anyone, or acknowledge greetings; he believed he ceased to exist from the time of the accident. He was a great help to Aunt Pauline around the house, cleaning or doing any necessary thing,

A breaker near Swoyersville, Pennsylvania. The flat surface in the foreground could be used as a playing field by neighborhood children. The author has a small patch of coal dirt in his right elbow, gained in a game of crack-the-whip on such a field more than half a century ago.

but speaking to no one but her, and very little of that.

If you looked carefully at Uncle George, you could see how handsome he must have been, and the damage to his face from the rock fall. When we knew him, he didn't really look much worse than most men who did brutal laboring work their whole lives. I felt very sorry for him, but he was far removed from caring about the sympathy of strangers, and I respected him in the privacy of his own little world.

An interesting footnote about this little town of Wyoming – the state of Wyoming was named after it. The Pennsylvania town was the scene of an Indian massacre in colonial days, the name being an adaptation of an Indian word meaning field or meadow.

The mine in which Uncle George was injured was a cruel one, and came into notoriety later. The miners dug a tunnel upwards into the Susquehanna River. When the river burst through, 12 of them perished instantly. Their bodies were never recovered, nor will they be. The river enlarged that opening, flooding that mine, and spread from tunnel to shaft to slope to vein through the underground network until it flooded mines twenty miles away. This calamity happened in January of 1959, now termed the Knox Mine Disaster, and virtually ended deep mining in the Northern Anthracite Coal Field. More than 7500 jobs were lost, with an annual payroll of $30,000,000.

The Army Corps of Engineers built a kind of coffer dam, or dike, around the opening, and constructed a rail line to the opening. Many gondola cars of cement and rock were pushed into the hole, but it took months to fill it up. Local miners, some of them, at any rate, don't believe it is stopped to this day.

Why would anyone dig into the river? Some said it was a mistake, others said it was the fault of racketeers and crooked union people who insisted the miners follow a rich vein of coal that led upwards to the river bottom. No matter what the cause, when the river came in, there was no hope of escape.

If Uncle George knew of this, no one ever found out. As far as he was concerned, the mine had killed him as a young man, and if it killed others later, that was of no consequence to him. A quarter century later, I took my little boy to see the place where the river went into the mine. You go back some side streets off the main street in the little town of Port Griffith, past semi-rural kind of houses, modern, neat, well-kept. I asked a neighbor where the exact spot was, and could anything still be seen? He replied that along the river bank there were yellow sulphur deposits from seepage from the mine, but that was all.

An almost-new looking brick rancher stood on the exact site where the mine buildings had been. From a hill behind it, it was possible to look down upon the railroad track bordering the river, and if you looked closely, the sulphur deposits along the river could be seen. What a scene of industry this had been two decades earlier; monstrous machines, floodlights through the night, huge pipes, battalions of men. All gone, now a pastoral scene of peace and tranquility, puzzling to my 10 year old son that I had brought him to this place to show him anything so ordinary. The miners were brave men, those who died, and those who live. I imagined that those who died would have wanted their community restored as it had been before the accident.

In a time of world energy problems, I couldn't help pondering how much harm, and how lasting it will be, was done to the mining industry. We'll know more about that in the next 10 or 20 years. Uncle George is gone; Aunt Pauline is gone; the 12 miners are gone, and the mine itself is gone. All the same, there were those who loved those people, and their memories are not gone, and that is important too.

The Mollie Maguires

My father's father was an Irishman. He lives in my speech when I talk with my older relatives. If I should say to my brother, "Get off me coat!" it would not be amiss or an affectation. My grandfather's father was a Mollie Maguire, as were his brothers. Great Grandfather John went to jail for over three years for being a Mollie. Upon his release he returned to work in the mines near Mahanoy City. Within a few months he was killed in a mine accident, that was thought by the relatives to be no accident. The power of the Mollies was destroyed by this time, and nothing ever came of it. Some books say the Mollies started in Scranton. This is probably not correct. Most likely they started in Ireland, and first became active around Mahanoy City.

To be a Mollie, you had to be Catholic, Irish, Hibernian, a miner, and be sponsored by a Mollie. It was a secret society, with an elaborate system of signs and passwords, which was organized to fight against the incredibly dangerous and oppressive working conditions in the mines. The Mollies were vigilantes who did much harm to the mine owners. The mine owners also did much harm to them. Around 1877, during the administration of President Rutherford Hayes, the Mollies played a principal role in the largest mass execution in the United States. There are many excellent and scholarly books and papers on the Mollies; this isn't one of them.

The first time I ever heard of the Mollies was from my mother, who detested my grandfather. The reputation of the Mollies was still so fearsome, 50 years later, that they were spoken of in hushed tones, with much ominous portent, as though one of them might be lurking under the kitchen table, or more likely, in the coal bin. As children, we heard of the Mollies who came for a mine superintendent, and not finding him at home, sat his wife on the hot coal stove to make her tell where he was. She really didn't know, and got her behind burned for nothing. This incident does not appear in any of the works that I have read about the Mollies.

That we were descended from Mollies on my father's side of the family was a real skeleton in the closet. My brother, who was reared with the grandfather, and still talks like him, would reply to questions about the Mollies with, "What do you want to know about those bums for? Better to forget them."

Many years later, in middle age, I decided to learn a little more about the Mollies, and see for myself if they were as bad as they were made out to be. First, I went to Mahanoy City, where the great grandfather and his brothers had lived. Mahanoy City is pronounced Mock-a-noy City, why, I don't know. It has a little note as the birthplace of the famous Dorsey brothers, Jimmy and Tommy, who had big bands in the 1930's. Their mother outlived them by many years, and died a few years ago in Mt. Carmel, a short distance from Mahanoy City.

A hundred years ago there was a small Catholic Church in Mahanoy City, which burned down. Whatever records there may have been are gone. I found some information about the grandfather in an old family Bible. It contained information about the grandfather and his brothers, also their wives. The ladies were named Nora, Bridget, and Kathleen, though I can't say who was married to who, all these years later. As dumb luck would have it, right at the time I was in Mahanoy City, there was a T.V. announcement about a memorial service for Jack Kehoe, the main leader of the Mollies. A century ago, Kehoe was hanged, along with 21 other men. The memorial service was held at the Pottsville Jail, where some of the hangings took place. Kehoe was pardoned by the Governor of Pennsylvania a hundred years later. It was proved that the evidence and trial were

10

JACK KEHOE'S
HIBERNIAN HOUSE
"THE MOLLY MAGUIRES"

Girardville, Pennsylvania

both wildly biased in favor of the mine owners, and he was hung on the basis of false testimony. No Catholics or miners were permitted to be on the jury, and the boundary of the area from which jurors could be selected was temporarily enlarged to bring in jurors from distant places. There were people on the jury who were deaf, and could not speak English. This trial had to be the low point in the history of American jurisprudence.

The great writer of Sherlock Holmes stories, Arthur Conan Doyle, also wrote a story based on his idea of the Mollies, which was entitled, "Valley of Fear." In this work, in which the Mollies are called "Scourers," the Mollies are depicted as evil incarnate. This story, while engrossing and fine literature, has nothing to do with the real story of the Mollies. Doyle was a passenger on an ocean liner with Frank Gowen, the principal mine owner in the trial, and got all his information from him. Gowen took his own life about ten years after the trial. The spy McParlan, who is depicted as a great hero in many accounts of the trials of the Mollies, was a self-serving scoundrel. He came to grief in Utah later on, when he tried to use his strike-breaking tactics there on the miners.

McParlan, in Utah, faced the great lawyer Clarence Darrow, in a trial of miners there. Darrow told him in court, "You caused the death of 22 miners in Pennsylvania, but you won't do it here," and he didn't, either. None of them were hung.

The jail in Pottsville is of surpassing ugliness. It exists today essentially as it was a hundred years ago. At the time of the memorial service for Jack Kehoe, my wife and I, along with our little boy, were given a tour of the facility. We were shown the cell in which Kehoe was confined for 18 months. There were rough, heavy planks on the floor, with a miniscule window to admit light. It looked like a medieval dungeon. The prisoner was spread-eagled on the floor, chained to

Pottsville Jail, Pennsylvania. Six Mollies were hanged here on June 21, 1877. The occasion was treated as a local celebration and drew a large crowd.

enormous iron rings. He was partially released to eat, or for bodily functions. The prisoner had the option of being spread-eagled face up or down, nothing else.

We met Kehoe's granddaughter, Alice Wayne, a most charming and friendly woman of late middle years. She still lives in the house once occupied by her grandfather, in Girardville, Pennsylvania. She had a wealth of information to share about the Mollies, and told us of many events in the area concerning them. A particularly vivid incident occurred at a nearby mine patch called "Wiggans," when the mine police came to the home of a suspected Mollie. These mine police were called "Modocs," and certainly matched the Mollies for evil. The man wanted had been warned the mine police were coming; and had left the house. In the confusion of the mine police trying to force their way into the house, with the housewife attempting to keep them out, the wife was shot and killed on the spot. The aged grandmother, witnessing this act, pulled the handkerchief down on the face of the mine policeman who did the slaying, and addressed him by name. The case never came to trial, nor were any charges placed. The event happened after the Mollies lost power, or the killer would not likely have survived.

The Mollies reached maximum influence between 1860 and 1870, gaining political strength in the 5 main anthracite coal mining counties. After the hangings, their power faded quickly. At best, they may not have numbered over 700 of many thousands of miners then employed. The Mollies are frequently given credit for being the beginning of the labor movement in the United States. This is probably not the case, though the time period involved is coincidental, and the Mollies were very forceful in supporting unions in the coal mines.

The Mollies did not show any of the usual manifestations of a cause or movement. One looks in vain for any

14

A miner's house in Eckley Village near Hazleton. This village is now maintained by the Pennsylvania Historical and Museum Commission. Various scenes in the film, "The Molly Maguires" were made at this location, in 1968.

literature, or espousal of social or economic philosophy, produced by the Mollies. There is very little of their writings that remain. Some of the writings are in the form of crude, frequently misspelled notes to mine supervisors warning them to leave the coal fields. Occasionally the notes were decorated with a death head or a coffin. If the person receiving the note left, he would survive. If he didn't he may well not have. One of the Mollies, while awaiting hanging, wrote a poem deploring the outcome of his life. It may be safe to say that anyone awaiting hanging would tend to deplore the outcome of his life.

The strength of the Mollies was coincidental with the formation of the labor movement in the United States. Another small enterprise of that period was the Pinkerton Detective Agency, of which the spy McParlan was an employee. The wealth accumulated from the mines was vast, and provided some of the capital used to develop the steel and railroad industries. This wealth, in the hundreds of millions of dollars, was not a part of the life of the miner. A few dollars a week was the best the miner could hope for, and a mule was valued above an Irishman. If I am in error in this comment, so was my grandfather, in that he made the comment many times in his life and I also heard it from other old miners. My older brother used to think it hilarious, when I was a small child, to tell me, "Pull in your ears, Brother, they're looking for mules down at the Cameron!"

My own conclusion about the Mollies is that they were a vigilante group who tried in their own way to look out for their own people. If any social good, in the sense of unions or better working conditions, sprung out of it, well and good, but I don't think that was the basic idea. One might well wonder, if mine conditions were so bad, why didn't the miners of other nationalities join the Mollies in their struggle?

We must look to history for some light on this. The mines were developed by British Protestant capitalists. The

16

The house of a mine superintendent at Eckley Village.
The supervisors of the miners were often Welsh or German.
The Welsh and Germans were needed for their knowledge of
the construction and operation of mines, which experience
they had acquired in their respective countries.

majority of the early mine laborers were wretchedly poor Irish immigrants, who fled the potato famine in Ireland in 1848. Each group brought with them the religious, political, and economic animosities which still make news in Ireland to the present time. Other national groups, Polish, Lithuanian, German, Italian, Slovak, and others, came after the first huge wave of Irish. By this time the unions were established, and the power of the Mollies was broken.

A roadside scene somewhere near Shenandoah. One does not have to look very far to find a culm bank in the hard coal regions.

The Legend of Lost Creek

This story is excerpted from "The Mollies Were Men" by Tom Barrett, and is presented by permission of the author.

A legend, with little foundation but much significance on the subject of "Justice" is contained in the tale of a captured Molly.

The "Sheet Iron" gang met at Fiddler's Green on Broad Mountain. The Molly lost his way and strayed into the camp. He was nabbed and immediately tied to a nearby tree and told to "make your peace with God, as you'll be burnt to a stake in the morning."

Meanwhile, a priest, on a sick call, was attracted by the bonfire. The bound man called to the clergyman and quickly made him aware of his awesome plight. The priest summoned the gang and protested.

After a hushed conference, a spokesman in the group announced that the Molly would get a "50-50" or "sportsman's chance" for his life. Two cards would be presented to him at dawn, one marked "Life" and the other "Death." His survival depended on his pick. A guard on duty just before dawn, whispered to the Molly: "My conscience bothers me. You don't have a chance. Both cards are marked "Death."

At sunrise the cards were placed face down on a tree stump, overlooking a swirling stream of water that disappeared quickly into wild, thick shrubbery. After a glance at the back of both cards, the prisoner suddenly reached out, picked up a card and threw it into the creek. In a moment the card was caught up in a twisting current and disappeared. The Molly turned to the priest and his captors and said, "That card in the creek is mine. If the one on the stump is marked "Death," the one I picked must be "Life."

Tradition has it that Lost Creek got its name from this

incident.

Editorial note: Lost Creek is a very small village near Shenandoah which exists to the present day.

The view approaching the little village of Lost Creek. All along the horizon there is a huge culm bank from decades of coal mining.

Pappy and the Big Mine Rats

My grandfather Eddie (on my father's side) always ate fish on Friday. He would have a sardine sandwich in his lunch pail, called a "jelly bucket," to refresh himself at lunch time. Dental care among miners 90 years ago wasn't much, and most older miners had false teeth, if they had any. Pappy had false teeth which he wore for cosmetic reasons, but for the serious business of eating, he removed them.

The mines had rats, big furry gray ones, that were tough and bold. The miners were tough, the mules were tough, and the rats were tough. It was a hard life. The rats got food the best way they could. Pappy got ready to eat his sardine sandwich one Friday, and removed his teeth. That quick, a large rat leaped up, grabbed the teeth, and ran off with them. Pap pursued the rat, while another one ate his sandwich. He never did get his false teeth back, nor did he get lunch that day, either.

This peculiar event pleased my mother greatly, and she delighted to tell of it, insisting the rat must have also wanted the teeth to eat the fish sandwich. Anything that bothered Pappy pleased her.

* * * * * * *

Upon reading the story of the "Mine Rats," I was reminded of a story my father tells of the dilemma of a mine rat trying to run off with a large hard-boiled egg in its shell. He could not fit it in his mouth, neither could he run and carry the egg at the same time. He scurried off, but soon returned with a companion. He laid on his back cradling the egg in his paws, while his companion grabbed hold of his tail with his teeth and dragged him away. I am always truly amazed at the ingenuity of so-called "inferior creatures."

The above anecdote contributed by Florence Mathews, of Shamokin.

The Importance of Mine Rats

When I mention rats in the mines, the present day reader may think this is another example of terrible working conditions. That's not how the miners looked at it – rats in the mine were regarded as valuable for mine safety. The rat and the canary were the best safety devices the early miners had.

My sister-in-law Anne told me that when she was young, the miners would say, "If you're having lunch and you're down to the last crumb, and you want that crumb, give it to the rat. The rat will save your life some day."

The rat is a small animal, and small animals can hear much higher-pitched sounds than humans. The rats could hear the mine timbers creaking long before humans could. Creaking timbers meant a cave-in might occur. If the rats began to leave an area, so would the miners. It is possible that rats could sense movement in the earth also. This could forewarn a collapse coming. Animals are known to sense earthquakes before humans.

I have read in old mining books that if the miners saw rats coming out of the mine as they came to work, that they would not enter until a complete safety inspection was made. I also heard that if a miner saw a red-headed woman as he went to work, he would turn around and go home. It was a serious bad omen. I sort of have my doubts about this one, if a mine village had a bunch of red-headed women, how would they ever get any work done?

The door boy, or nipper, seated at his solitary post. The rat might be his only companion through the long lonely hours in the darkness. He could go to work at the age of 9 or 10. He would receive 11¢ an hour for a ten to twelve hour work day. By the age of 14 or 15 he could become a driver boy, taking the place of the regular mule driver when needed. The door boy opened and closed the mine doors to let the mule-drawn mine cars pass through.

Nora, the widow of John McKeever. The picture of
Nora was drawn from a description of Nora by my mother,
who did not like her. Other than the Irish clay pipe, I doubt if
she looked any different than any other older women of that
time and place. John and his brothers James and William were
Mollies. John and James lived in Mahanoy City a century ago
and they were mentioned in Tom Barrett's book, "The Mollies
Were Men." Both John and William died in mine accidents.

The Fireboss

Pap McKeever was a fireboss, a job of considerable responsibility. While all jobs in the mine were dirty, dreadful and laborious, some were worse than others. The fireboss had the authority to assign men under him to their places of work. Upon his assignment, you might stand up to work, or crawl on your hands and knees. This would be for ten or twelve hours in a coal seam three feet high.

The fireboss entered the mine several hours before the workers. He went through every section to look for safety hazards of any kind. Weak timbers, loose rock overhead, methane or carbon dioxide gas (the first explodes, the second suffocates), were among the hazards he investigated. He had a crude little office in the mine tunnel, called a peg shanty. It got its name from the pegboard by the door, on which the miners moved a peg by their name as they came to work. At the end of the work day, if a miner did not move his peg to the original position, the other miners had to search for him. It could happen that he was in a narrow seam that came down on him.

I have heard two explanations of the term "fireboss." The first one was that if a miner did not produce 3 carloads of coal per day, 15 tons, that on the third day he was fired. The fireboss did the firing, hence, "fireboss." The other explanation was that as the fireboss made his lonely safety rounds, if he encountered a pocket of methane, the safety lantern could ignite it and it would flash in his face. This left characteristic purplish burns, so this was also given as the origin of "fireboss."

This is a peg shanty, the office of the fireboss. It was a crude opening dug in solid rock, and faced with cinder block and a doorway. It contained a desk, chair, and safety equipment. It was located deep in the mine on the main tunnel.

The Fireboss of the Mine

(1)
I am a fireboss of the mine
  of that you are aware
My duty to my fellow-men
  I do with every care
I leave my bed at an early hour
  while the world enjoys its sleep
And wind my way to the mine alone
  in wind, rain, snow or sleet.

(2)
And as I enter the dreary mine
  my heart, I raise in prayer
And ask the Almighty to protect me
  and the men and boys in my care
I examine first the intake
  the main blood vein of the coal
And see if the air is going
  towards the out-let, its last goal.

(3)
I go along the gangway with
  my safety lamp in hand
I examine the road, the roof and side
  and the current from the fan
Then at the face I raise my lamp
  carefully to test for gas,
I examine the top, the timber and prop,
  and the manner in which they blast.

(4)
I examine each place for CH_4
  also for CO_2
I never found any CO
  or H_2S that burns so blue
I examine the chutes and headings
  and the breasts upon the pitch
Every man gets my attention
  even the man that digs the ditch.

(5)
I note the dangers of every place
  the ribs, the face, the top
I tell the men if its right or wrong
  the way they stand their prop
As I go up and down the breasts
  the dangers alone I face
I leave my mark behind to show
  that I was in every place.

(6)
I examine all the wagon breasts
  by my duty I am lead
To every working place were men
  must earn their daily bread
I always look for danger
  as all alone I brave
While going through the workings
  my fellow-men to save.

(7)
Then I return to my station
  so tired, fatigued within
And as the men arrive one by one
  my daily troubles begin
I must tell the men in No. 1
  to be sure to stand that prop
I must tell the men in No. 2
  to take down that piece of top.

(8)
I must tell the men in No. 3
  to drive a heading to No. 2
I must tell the men in No. 4
  to drive their heading through
I must tell the men in No. 5
  they will surely have some gas
Unless they keep the menway closed
  to the face before they blast.

(9)
I must tell them of all the dangers
  to be as careful as they can
That "Safety First" is for them
  and for their fellow-man
Then I meet the Company men
  and tell them what to do
I go and sign my daily report
  and my mornings work is through.

(10)
Then I sit down to eat my piece
  one half an hour I take
Until I am on the go again
  my second round to make
I go to the place most dangerous
  to the place I know danger lies
And see that the men work safely
  for themselves, their children and
    their wives.

(11)
And if a man meets with an accident
  or killed perchance, you know
That this does sometimes happen
  as along through life we go
Don't condemn unless there's a reason
  was he shot or did the roof cave
For its little does the public know
  of the lives and limbs I save.

(12)
I have told you the life of a Fireboss
  his trials and troubles aren't few
True he receives his wages
  Doesn't the door-boy receive his too?
Ah no, there's higher motive
  and proudly his flag he can wave
For his duty is high and noble
  his fellow-man to save.

(13)
And at last when life is over
  and my soul to its maker flies
To be judged, receive sentence according
  to works done on this world of sighs
I expect to hear the consoling words
  from teh Sacred Lips of Thine
"Well done good and faithful servant
  thou fireboss of the mine."

Written by James E. Brennan
Fireboss Richards #4 Colliery
circa 1897

Copyright by Ann Marie DeBolt
Grandaughter
November 12, 1993

Suggested by John C. Brennan
Grandson
Bethlehem, PA

Canals and Coal

Grammy's dad worked on canal boats. He was not the captain, but he didn't have the lowliest job either He was a handsome fellow, always had to be called Uncle Dick. He was sensitive about aging and wouldn't permit grandchildren to call him Grandpa. My mother didn't think much of Uncle Dick. She said he only came home long enough to make a baby, then you wouldn't see him for another year. After 7 babies, he was real slow to come home. All the same, he was good about sending money home for the family, they never complained about being in need. Uncle Dick was a musician, a cornet player, and when the canals were frozen in winter, he had a band called Gilham's Big Six in which he travelled and made money.

Two of the 7 babies turned out to be miners, Neil and Floyd. Floyd I never knew, he was the one that got killed in the mine fan long before I was born. Neil I knew in childhood, he always had a smile on his face. He dearly wanted to be the life of the party, he just wasn't very good at being funny. When he told a joke, he would mangle the punch line, or forget it altogether.

His wife, Laura, was a big heavy lady of most somber disposition, you never saw her smile. When Neil would tell one of his awful jokes, everyone would laugh just as nice as if it really was funny, except Laura. We all knew he meant to be funny. Laura would give him a mournful stare and say, "Now, now, Neil." It didn't mean a thing to him, five minutes later he'd do it again.

Neil must have loved Laura, they had children and were married a very long time. For having the hard life of a miner, Neil always had an amazingly cheerful disposition.

An old print showing canal boats and freight cars being loaded with coal at Mauch Chunk (now Jim Thorpe) on the Lehigh Canal.

Pre-canal transportation in Pennsylvania was by Flat-Boat or "Ark" floating downstream, usually on a spring "freshet."

The Mean Mule and the Driver Boy

One of the guides at the Scranton Museum Mine Tour had worked in that mine as a young man. He told of a miner he knew who was old when he was young – this man had worked in the mine when mules were used. The man who told the story was not the driver boy, but he knew the person who was in this particular incident.

The driver boy was leading the mule through a somewhat narrow passage, when the mule began to squash him against the wall. The driver boy was pinned, and did not have room to swing his whip. As the mule kept squeezing, the driver boy in desperation used the handle of his whip to hit the mule over the head. He was a very strong boy, and killed the mule with the blow.

The foreman was called, and viewing the dead mule, said to the driver boy, "You kin go home now."

"Ahh, an' when do I come back t'work?" asked the boy.

"You kin come back t'work when'at mule comes back t'life." said the foreman.

Anyone responsible for injury, much less death, to a mule was fired on the spot. No excuse, no explanation, no recourse, just go. I mentioned this incident to my older brother Dick recently. He in turn told me of a man he worked with as a young man, who had also been a mule driver. I know the man's name, in this story we will call him John.

John was guiding his mule in backing a dinky car up a little tipple to dump it. The mule went too far, and instead of dumping, the car went right over and pulled the mule with it into a hole maybe 12 feet or more deep. John was petrified. If the mule was hurt, it was the end of his job. He quickly crawled down the hole and checked over the mule, which did not seem to be too bad off for the drop.

The foreman was not around, but a few other workers had seen what happened and came to John's aid. One of them quickly got a sling, which they placed around the mule, and with another mule pulled the first one out of the hole. The mule which had gone down the hole had some cuts and scratches, but was otherwise none the worse for wear. John had some black salve handy, which was sort of a cure-all for mules. He put it on the cuts and they hardly even showed. Black salve was just that, a black salve that smelled something of creosote, I never did know what was in it.

John was so pleased that the mule was unharmed he stated, "Fer the next two weeks, me'nat mule was brothers. What I got, he got."

By this John meant that he shared any goodies in his lunch with the mule. If a mule driver was fond of his beast, he might feed it candy, sugar, figs, apples or dates. Drivers who chewed tobacco, and many of them did, would cut off a big piece, called a "quid," for the mule. In the very early days, on occasion the driver would bring two bottles of beer in the morning, one for him and one for the mule (There is no record of whether the mule worked any better on this diet.).

When my brother was a child, Pappy Eddie took him to the Bear Valley Colliery where he worked as a fireboss. They still had mules in the early thirties, and Pap took Dick to see the mules when they were brought up from the mines periodically. They were brought up to give them fresh air and sunlight. The mules would go into a frenzy of delight when they got into the corral. They would roll in the dust and kick their legs in the air, and they would stand on their heads. They would rear up on their hind legs, and whinney and neigh as loud as they could. This performance would last maybe a half hour until they exhausted themselves in celebration. They only stayed up for the day, then back down again.

Mule driver boy, circa, 1890. If he was 15, he might have already been working 7 years full time. "and made them men before they could be boys," John M. Powderly.

The Little Boy in the Neilsen Shaft

Mines have shafts that go deep into the earth, also slopes that lead off from the shafts, which is how the veins of coal lie. Above the shafts of the larger mines are buildings holding machinery to work the cables for cages, fans for the air, and breakers to separate the coal into different sizes. These places, to a child, were grim, ugly, and fascinating. Sometimes they had watchmen who would chase the children away. It was potentially very dangerous for a child, but if a child got inside, it was a daring thing to tell the other children, so naturally they went in once in a while.

In the winter of 1941, possibly around Christmas, I heard fire trucks going down the street, and followed them. In a small town, you could always find out where they went easily. They went to the Neilsen Colliery, where a crowd had gathered, but there was no fire. People said some kids had been in there playing, and one of them had fallen into the shaft. Sure enough, one of them did. The shaft was filled with water, 1200 feet deep. The Neilsen no longer worked because of flooding, and it did not have a watchman. The firemen put hoses into the shaft to make the water circulate, and the next day they got the boy out.

As a child, I had gone sleigh-riding (sledding; sledding was called sleigh-riding invariably, though in my entire childhood I never once saw an actual horse and sleigh) on the hill behind the Neilsen Colliery. I didn't know if I knew the boy or not, but went to the viewing anyway, mostly for curiosity to see if I did know him. Children are beautiful when they are sleeping. He looked like he was sleeping, all dressed up ready to go to church. We were all children of the mine country. We knew of air holes and abandoned shafts. Death in the mines could greet a child as quickly as the parent. This was what made playing around in them exciting. Later on the Neilsen burned, and it's all gone now.

The Uncle and the Roman Candle

Many of the men on my father's side of the family were very heavy drinkers when they got the chance. On my mother's side, several of her brothers were also heavy drinkers. One of them, who died before I was born, got drunk at a Fourth of July picnic, where fireworks were the featured attraction. This particular uncle thought it was great fun to walk around with a Roman Candle in his mouth, spouting flames to the amazement of onlookers. Not all Roman Candles work in the way they should; sometimes they squirt out the back. This one did, and it went down his neck. He talked like a bullfrog after that. I'm not sure anymore, but I think that when he was still a young man, he was working underneath of a car, when it fell on him and squashed him.

Winter scene. Trolley line between Centralia and Mt. Carmel, PA. About 1900.

When Pappy Got Buried

Both of my male grandparents were called Pap, or Pappy, by the grandchildren. Pappy (Grandpa Bert) on my mother's side was very different from the Pappy (Grandpa Eddie) on my father's side. Grandpa Bert was English and Protestant, Grandpa Eddie was Irish Catholic. The antagonisms vexing Ireland at this time seem to me an echo of the prejudices and antagonisms that I heard in the mine country a half century ago.

Pappy (Grandpa Bert) had started out as a breaker boy at the age of 9, in the breaker across the street from the house where I was born. In those days, a miner would start as a breaker boy at the age of 9 or 10, go into the mines around 15, developing miner's asthma over the next 25 years, then slowly suffocate for the next 10 or 15 years. It was the pattern of the miner's life.

Pappy had only gone to second grade in school, and though he was a naturally bright and talented man, did not so regard himself. He saw himself as a miner only, and he worked with dynamite. If the powder charge did not explode, it was his job to see why. Someone had to do it.

There was a movie around that time, "How Green Was My Valley," about miners in Wales, and in the movie there was a big mine explosion. I saw the movie, and mentioned it to my mother, who said Pap had gotten buried several times. The next time I saw Pap, I inquired if this was so, how often, how long, what it was like, and so forth. He listened to my questions with a solemn good humor that was a characteristic of this man. He wasn't a cheerful sort of a fellow, but he wasn't ill-humored like Pappy Eddie.

"Hey Pap, Mom said you was buried a couple of times when you was in the mines. Is that right?"

"Yeah, that's right."

"Well, how long was you buried?"

Inside of this building was a large rotary machine that turned the dinky cars upside down to dump the coal. It was then carried to the top of the breaker to be cleaned and sorted. At the turn of the century breaker boys, aged 8 to 14, worked 9 hours a day, picking slate and rock from the coal. My grandfather Bert was a breaker boy.

"Maybe about a week. I was trapped a couple of times."

"Was you scared, Pap?"

"I was plenty scared."

"What did you do?"

"We prayed a lot, me and the other lads. There was nothin' else you could do."

"Didn't you get out of the mines after that?"

"Naw, I belonged in the mines. That's all I know."

Pap had been an incredibly strong man in youth. While of average height, he wore a 17 1/2 collar, and had a slim waist. When I knew him, he was gaunt and stooped, coughing and wheezing. It took him twenty minutes to get up the steps from the cellar with a bucket of coal. He had to rest on every step to try to gasp some oxygen into what was left of his lungs.

When Pap was younger, his son, my Uncle Charl, got a job at the Briggs and Stratton plant somewhere in, or around, Detroit. He became a foreman, and once after Pap had been entombed and rescued, invited him out to Detroit. Charl said he would give Pap an easy job on the assembly line where Charl was a foreman. Pap went to Detroit, and sat on the assembly line for several weeks. One day, he came to Charl and said, "Charl, I know you're trying to do a good thing for me, but I'm going back home. I belong in the mines. This is women's work here." With that, he left, and returned to the mines at Shamokin.

As a miner, Pap knew who he was. By doing the dangerous job, he held the respect of his fellow miners. On the assembly line, he felt diminished. Back in the mines, he knew who he was. Not everyone is so fortunate.

Towards the end of his life, the landlord of the house Pap rented came to him one day and said, "Bert, you've been a good tenant for years. I'm gonna die soon, and I have no family. Take the house, I'm giving it to you."

A general view of the Cameron Colliery, conveying the enormous size of the culm bank surrounding it, the largest in the world. I know that the Cameron was called Glenburn and other names during its long history, but it was the Cameron when Grandpa Bert worked there, and it will always be the Cameron to me.

To which Pap replied, "Oh, no, I couldn't do that. There are legal things in owning a house. I have no education, and couldn't handle all that. Thank you all the same."

Pap and his wife reared 8 children. He did the blasting job for years. Despite this, he didn't believe that he could accept ownership of a small frame rowhouse. Incredible. Pap died Christmas eve, 1948, at home surrounded by relatives. He was a good man, and I wish I had known him better.

Railroad tracks to the quarry and bum's camp. The Cameron Colliery is to the right. The children would occasionally hitch rides on slow-moving trains, though this was regarded as very dangerous and rarely done. A fast passenger train came along the left-hand track each day at 5:30 p.m.

The Fire in the Cameron

When I was little, my Grandpa Bert told me that the Cameron was on fire, as well as other mines in the neighborhood. I knew he didn't mean the breaker, since when breakers caught on fire, that was the end of them. He meant there was a fire in the mine, and it had been burning for many years. This was a mystery and a marvel to me, and I have to admit that I didn't really believe him.

Anthracite coal isn't the easiest thing in the world to get on fire, as you can find out by trying to start a fire when the furnace has gone out. You need some paper, some small sticks, and some larger ones. Maybe in 15 minutes you can get it started pretty good. Once started, it is a very hot fire. If the draft isn't set right, it will burn with a rhythmic whooshing sound that is surprisingly noisy. This means it's burning too fast and needs to be dampened.

The right way to dampen it is to adjust the flue, or dampener. Children don't always do things the right way, and a few times my brother and I tried dampening it with a garden hose. It doesn't quite cause a real explosion, but you get a blast of steam and ash out of the furnace door that will make you think twice before you do it again.

Mines are wet. Almost all the big ones need pumps to get the water out. Besides this, the veins of coal are under hundreds of feet of earth, or embedded in rock, which requires dynamiting. How in the world could coal under water, earth, or in rock continue to burn? This question puzzled me to no end as a child. It puzzles the U.S. Corps of Engineers and many other learned experts all these years later. Many millions of dollars have been expended to put out some of these fires without success. Grandpa Bert was right, the Cameron was on fire 50 years ago. He said it was on fire a hundred years ago, when he was a small child. The fires can travel for miles underground, going deeper, were sometimes coming to the surface, depending upon how the veins of coal lie that are burning.

Some years back, when I visited Shamokin, I saw wisps of smoke drifting from the top of the culm bank. It was high enough that it did not pose a hazard to the residents of the community. About the same time, I visited relatives near Wilkes-Barre, and saw where fires had come to the surface on the outskirts of town. Some residents had to be evacuated, their homes standing there abandoned and forlorn. A high wire fence surrounded the area to keep children out.

The burning seams of coal are a serious problem in the coal country. Whether a small town like Centralia, or a fair-sized city like Wilkes-Barre, they are alike subject to the possibility of burning veins coming up to the surface, or long before they do this, sending up poisonous gases. Underground burning coal seams are persistent and resistant beyond belief. Water, mud, concrete, excavating, and other techniques are used in attempts to contain them. Sometimes they do, and sometimes they don't.

When I was a little boy, and asked Pappy why they didn't put them out, his answer was simple and direct, "Because they can't." It appears he knew whereof he spoke, and you can go to Centralia today to confirm his observation.

Centralia has recently been in the news because of the coal vein burning under the town, causing some families to leave their homes. Other homes have gas gauges in them to monitor the level of carbon monoxide in the air, which can kill quietly and quickly. The town is suffused with the smell of burning sulfur, noticeable when you first enter the town. After a little while, it seems to fade.

The fire started about 50 years ago at a trash dump on the edge of town. An outcropping of the coal seam reached the surface there, and became ignited from burning trash.

When the coal fire was first noticed, the local mining company was approached to put it out. They said it was for the state to do. When the state was approached, they said it was too big, and for the federal government to do. Several years had gone by, permitting the fire to spread underground. Now the federal government says the fire is too big to try to extinguish, and that the people affected should move away. It is their home town, and they don't want to move. Many of the people are up in years, and couldn't afford to move even if they wanted to . The fire has spread a mile or more from the original site. The federal government did place hundreds of vent pipes into the burning seam to carry off gases.

Centralia sits above a coal bed estimated to contain as much as 40 million tons of coal, or more. The price of coal varies markedly with the availability of oil, but at a price of $100 per ton, this coal may be valued at hundreds of millions of dollars. All these figures may be wildly erroneous, but of a certainty, the coal beneath the town represents immense wealth. Unlike the coal near Wilkes-Barre and Scranton, it is not flooded as the coal beds are there. There is one small mine operating in Centralia today, producing a very high quality of anthracite.

Since the above comments were written in 1981, extensive changes have taken place in Centralia. A governmental agency, the Columbia County Redevelopment Authority, has been established to assist those families wishing to relocate to nearby communities. Mr. William Klink, the director of the agency, advises that only a few families now remain. When these families relocate, Centralia will be only a coal region memory. To my knowledge, it is the only community to have to be abandoned because of a coal fire.

Breastwork opening of a bootleg hole a mile and a half from Centralia, Pennsylvania. Heat from the burning coal has burned off all vegetation above, and lightened the rocks above the opening.

One of hundreds of vent pipes into the burning coal seam at Centralia. The town is in the background. These vent pipes smoke a little sometimes, and some of them bring up an astounding amount of heat.

A small mine still operating within the city limits of Centralia, Pennsylvania, 1981. The miners here were proud of their work, and of the high quality of coal obtained from this mine.

Editorial note: This mine no longer operates. It was closed after the picture was taken.

Peacock Coal, Sulfur Diamonds, and Air Holes

What did poor children do for amusement in the 1930's? You could go for a walk, or might find a few buddies and go for a walk and potato roast. All that was required were a few kitchen matches, some salt, and a couple of potatoes, easily carried in the pockets. I have no idea anymore of what potatoes sold for in 1938. Milk was 6 cents a quart, bread was 6 cents a loaf, a hotdog or a hamburger with everything was a nickel.

Potatoes were easy to come by; everyone had some at home. With a couple of friends and a nice day, though it didn't matter if it was a nice day or not, the poor children of the 1930's, were not used to conveniences, you could walk out of town a few miles and have a potato roast. Favored places were the bum's camp, the cave, and the quarry. The bum's camp had a beautiful small clear free-running spring, that even if you muddied it up it would clean itself in a few minutes.

In the 30's, there really were bums who traveled on the railroad, dropping off the trains outside of the town to work or panhandle a bit before moving on. The bum's camp was a pretty little glade a short distance from the railroad track, used by those unfortunates. Occasionally, a bum might be seen lying around the bum's camp, or in the cave not far away, but we did not disturb them, nor was there any concern for their welfare. We were children, they were adults, what they did was their own affair.

When I was old enough to go on walks out of town, maybe 8 or 9, my mother warned me about air holes. "If you go down an air hole, nobody will ever know, they'll never find you, and you'll never be seen again."

Air holes were the collapsed remnants of bootleg mines. The mountains surrounding the coal mining towns were pocked with many such places, in that bootlegging had been practiced as long as regular mining. Miners working the regular mines would gain a knowledge of the location of productive seams, and with a few companions, would set up shop for themselves, digging the coal, carrying it away, and selling it. They paid no taxes or royalties, nor did they obtain legal permission to mine, which is why they were called bootleggers.

If the mining operation remained very small, and the miners were discreet, they could do this for several years before being stopped by the land owner or company holding mineral rights. Once the mine got deep enough to require an old car engine to pull up the coal, it was big enough to be closed up, or the miners would abandon it rather than face legal actions.

Mines do not all go straight down into the ground. Some do, some are on a slant (called a slope) and some are horizontal. The dangerous abandoned ones were those that went straight down. A decade or two after abandonment, the tops fell in, making a funnel-shaped depression. In the summer they were easy to spot, since the funnel-shaped depression was very noticeable, and it was always surrounded by coal dirt and slate. When the tops fell in, they would cover the shaft, though there might only be a relatively small amount of material filling in the hole, with a deep shaft under it.

You did not play in air holes. Mom's injunction was not a "Bogey man will get you" kind of thing. The weight of a child could break through the debris covering the top of the shaft, with a drop of one or two hundred feet into the water in the shaft, with the debris raining down on you from above. You would not survive, and if you were by yourself, you wouldn't be found either, most likely. You learned where the air holes were in the summer, and if you walked through the area in winter when snow was on the ground, you made sure you went around them. Not all air holes had collapsed tops. Sometimes we threw rocks into them to see how long it took to hit the water in them. For some of them it took a long time.

Peacock coal is an artifact of anthracite. Impurities in the coal cause it to be iridescent, with a wild and brilliant array of colors, appearing and disappearing as the piece is turned. In the 30's it was regarded as a nuisance, not being the purest form of coal, and was picked out to be thrown away, though it seemed to burn as well as the rest of the coal in which it appeared. A few years ago, I wanted to obtain a piece for my son, so I went to the house in which I was born, to inquire of the man who lives there. He is in the coal trucking business to this day, and his children were my playmates at one time. I asked him if he had any laying around, or where I could get some. He told me it was rarely found anymore, and he had not seen any for years. I asked if he would inquire of the miners he knew to look out for a piece for me, and he said he would. I promised to pay him whatever someone might ask for it. What I offered to pay was what 3 truckloads of coal sold for in the 30's, or the truck itself in bad condition. He never could get any, though.

All to no avail. I went to a little shop in Shamokin offering coal souvenirs and asked for something made of peacock coal. The lady wanted to be helpful, and finally found one item with some very faint traces of blue and gold in it. If you knew what you were looking for and looked real hard, using some imagination, you could almost make it out. Why peacock coal should be so rare anymore I don't know. There is plenty of coal still there, as the mine fires show us so plainly, so there must still be some peacock coal around somewhere.

The trade of sulphur diamond cutter probably does not exist anymore. There was one of them who lived about a block away from our house, who eked out a marginal living by producing jewelry items made from sulphur diamonds. He was a Negro who was married to a white lady, which was most uncommon in those days. Old Henry was a kind and gentlemanly person, always nice to us children, and respectful to everyone. His wife was a different story altogether. She was none too bright, and possessed of an incredibly bad temper. More than once she was known to have chased him out of the house and up the street with a hatchet. We never knew what he did to deserve such a display of anger, but it was thought that his wife was a little crazy, and maybe that was the problem.

Sulphur diamonds are a form of iron pyrite, or fools' gold. It is grainy and crystalline in appearance, and takes a nice polish. Miners finding a lump of it would bring it to Henry, who would pay a small sum. Then he would cut it and polish it, placing it in rings or lockets. These he sold, also for a small sum. Many miners had a ring or something made of this material. I still have grandfather Eddie's ring, which must be 90 years old or more.

If the Hearse Came Down Market Street

At the turn of the century, when my mother was a girl, horse drawn transportation was the normal means. There were horse drawn hearses in those days. An accident in the mines was made known by the blowing of mine whistles, and train whistles.

This was the signal for women and children to come out of their homes and line the street as the wagons brought the victims back into town. As each wagon would pass, the women would anxiously inquire of whom it contained. When the hearse came along, the process was repeated, with each family dreading to find that it contained a father, son or brother. In this awesome lottery, someone had to get the bad news.

It was better to find that a relative was not in the hearse than that he was. If he was still trapped in the mine, there was a chance he could be rescued. For those who perished, the calamity to the family was of a degree hard to imagine today. There was no welfare, no social services, no survivors insurance. A collection would be taken up in the neighborhood, and this pitifully small sum would go largely to providing a funeral for the deceased. The loss of the family breadwinner meant that the male children would go to work as slate pickers at the breakers around the age of 9 or 10. Female children might go to work in the textile mills which were then in operation, perhaps at the age of 12 or 13. Old folks would go to the poorhouse, or County Almshouse, as it was called.

The names of the social institutions at the time seem foreign and remote with the passage of time. There was the pest house, an isolated building to house those with serious communicable diseases. There was the school for the feeble-minded, and an epileptic colony. The state mental institution was called the nut house by everyone, including those of education, in colloquial speech.

My mother was among those who lined Market Street on the occasions when the wagons and hearse made their dreary journeys. The quiet terror of those vigils lived still in her voice decades later when Pappy (Grandpa Bert) was removed by black lung from the peril of the mine, to cough away his remaining days. He never complained.

Lovely woodland scene at Tuscarora State Park near Mahanoy City, Pennsylvania.

INTERLUDE

Coal mining was, and is, a very dangerous occupation. A reader of these stories might think that I exaggerated the hazard involved. Not so, as I talked with relatives who were descended from miners, or who had been miners themselves, I was shocked at the number of deaths and injuries they could recount from their own personal experience. In brief, I will summarize the experience of various relatives.

My granduncle William was killed in the mines near Mahanoy City. My grandfather Bert was buried alive several times. My wife's father, Mike, was injured. Her brother, George, was injured. Her Uncle Peter was killed in the mines near Pittston. My wife's brother Casimir, was married to a lady from Pittston whose father was seriously injured in an accident in which 3 of her uncles died. The father of my brother-in-law, Alex, was seriously burned in an explosion near Exeter. My wife's Uncle George, was injured and disfigured.

My brother-in-law George worked in the mine at Inkerman, near Pittston, in 1941. He had a Lithuanian friend about 10 years older than himself. The Lithuanian fellow recounted how, in the 1920's, two men brought the body of his father to their home. They knocked on the door, and when it was opened by the mother, laid the corpse on the living room floor. They announced he had been killed in a rock fall, and without another word, departed. This tragedy, and variations of it, were repeated many times over the years, in mining families.

In a century of mining, 35,000 miners perished in the anthracite coal regions of Pennsylvania. Some mines averaged as high as 4 deaths per year for every year of operation.

My wife's home town was Pittston, my own was Shamokin, Pennsylvania. Let me pose a curious question at this point; What have Shamokin, Pittston, Mexico City, Nagasaki, Glasgow, and Dortmund (Germany) in common? They are all the sites of mine disasters in which miners lost their lives. Reference: "Darkest Hours" by Jay Robert Nash. In the section "Major Mine Disasters" found in this book, literally hundreds of places, some famous, most unknown, are recorded as the location of mine disaster.

I would think that living in an environment where sudden death or injury was a commonplace fact of life would have some sort of psychological impact on the inhabitants, though I am not at all sure of just what it might be. When I was young, in the 1940's, Girardville, Pennsylvania, was reputed to have the most bars per capita in the United States. I have no idea as to the accuracy of this, but of certainty the coal towns had an abundance of saloons, one on every corner in the business sections. There was a corresponding large number of churches to serve those of every nationality and faith. The bars were patronized by the miners, the churches by their wives. The wives prayed first for the safety of their husbands in the mines, and second, for their husbands to spend less time in the bars. It was said of miners, "They worked hard, they played hard, and they died hard." This bit of homespun philosophy sums up their lives as well as anything else I've heard.

Pappy and the Pledge

Grandpa Eddie was what used to be called a "good drinking man" on occasion. What this meant was that once a year, when his pledge was up, he would go on a monumental binge that would last several days. Grammy didn't take kindly to these binges.

When I was very small, my Mom would tell us children when Pap was on his annual tear. She took a perverse satisfaction in this, in that she liked to criticize Pap for anything she could. According to Mom's description, Pap would go from bar to bar until he could barely walk. Pap was Catholic and Grammy was Protestant, so the church ladies from Grammy's church who saw Pap would pass the word along concerning how he was and which bar he was in. My Mom called these ladies the "missionaries," who kept Grammy posted on Pap's progress, or lack of it.

Pap was a big man, very strong, and with a bad temper to boot. Nevertheless, Grammy had no fear of him when he was drunk. She was a tiny lady, probably not over 5 feet, and not heavy at all. The drunker he got, the madder she got. When the missionaries brought word that he was finally on his way home, Grammy would wait on the front porch with a broom. He would stagger from tree to tree coming up Market Street, with Grammy waiting patiently. There were about 7 or 8 wide steps coming up to the front porch. When Pap tried to come up the steps, Grammy would beat him back down with the broom. After she had abused him sufficiently, she would permit him to crawl up to bed on his hands and knees. He would sleep it off, and go to the priest the next day, at which time he would take the pledge for another year.

On his last binge, a few years before he died, when he got to bed Grammy took all his clothes off. It was an old fashioned bed, a brass four-poster style, of sturdy manufacture. Grammy got some clothes line, and tied him spread-eagle face down, very secure.

"Eddie, you're too drunk now to feel a good beatin', but you're gonna get it good tomorrow when you wake up," Grammy told him. Sure enough, she waited till the next morning. Pap was in the throes of a mighty hangover when she came in the room with a heavy leather belt. She proceeded to turn him red from top to bottom. Pap was too incapacitated to do anything but threaten her, which he did. "Katie, when I get loose from here I'm gonna kill you!"

To which she answered, "No, and you ain't neither." There was something about the way she said it that made him pause and think a while.

"Why ain't I?"

"Cause I sent for the priest, and you ain't a'gettin outta there till he comes. So you might just as well shut up, or I'll beat you some more."

Pap stayed right there, since there was nothing else he could do. The priest came, and Grammy made Pap take the pledge while he was still tied up, then she untied him. He took the pledge for a year, which was all he ever did, but his health failed after that, and when the year was up, he didn't drink. If he ever drank any more until he died, it wasn't enough to notice.

Pap died when I was still a small child, so I don't really have much memory of him. He was a good violinist, and played a great deal when he was younger. Maybe that was what attracted Grammy to him.

Ginger Snaps and Walnut Cookies

Grandpa Bert lived in a small wooden row house, perched on a steep hill. If you stood on the front porch of a house, you could look down on the next door neighbor's porch, and on the roof of the 3rd or 4th neighbor's porch. The sidewalks were a series of steps, 2 steps and a flat spot about 4 feet, and 2 more steps. You learn to run them in sequence, step, step, jump, step, step, and so on.

Grandpa Bert (Pappy) had a little brownish tan terrier dog named Ginger. It was a female dog, nervous and excitable, but very pretty as dogs go. Ginger was an odd dog, who ran up to you in what appeared to be a friendly manner, but if you put your hand down to greet her, you got bit. Ginger snapped. This was considered hilarious by all the relatives, but it was in an era when law suits were almost unheard-of. In this present era of instant litigation, Ginger would be a luxury or pest, both, and impossible to keep.

Pap's first wife was a lady named Rebecca Goldman. Her father had been a Union soldier in the Civil War. He was captured by the Southern troops and placed in the notorious Andersonville prison in Georgia, and was one of the small number of survivors of this dreadful place. When we were small children, my father took us to Gettysburg and pointed out his regiment's name on one of the numerous memorial monuments there. Rebecca died of leukemia before I was born.

Pap's second wife was a big heavy lady we called Aunt Mame. She was a pleasant soul who liked to bake cookies. Pap's contribution to this endeavor was to bash walnuts for the cookies. He would get a brick and some newspaper and a big hammer and smash the walnuts, then extract the nutmeats for the cookies. His eyesight had failed, and he was not so expert at separating the shells from the nuts.

He was very sensitive about his failing eyesight, and it

was considered very poor form in the family to say anything about finding a piece of walnut shell in the cookies.
The walnut cookies were delicious, and once you knew to
watch out for stray shells, it posed no problem for hungry
children.

The other Grandpa, Eddie, made root beer of a most
amazing power. The root beer was mixed up in the kitchen,
poured into bottles, which were then capped with a hand-
operated machine. This was then placed in the cellar to age.
When it blew some of the caps off, it was considered
suitable to drink. Hard to say, all these years later, which
was more fun, drinking the stuff, or squirting each other
with it when the caps were pulled off. We would open the
bottles in the alley beside the house, and it would squirt ten
feet.

Miners in the Civil War

Pennsylvania coal miners took part in a very odd battle of the Civil War, the "Battle of the Crater." One thing miners are good at above all, and that's digging holes and tunnels. This ability was put to use in an attempt to break the siege of Petersburg. This was toward the end of the war, the last year. General Robert Lee and his forces occupied the city of Petersburg, Virginia, and surrounded it with very strong fortification. This was near Richmond, the capitol of the Confederacy, which Lee could also protect with his strong army. The Union Army, under General Ulysses Grant, faced an impossible task to break through the Southern defenses. In a frontal attack, the losses to the Union forces would be unbearable.

In the Union Army there was a group of coal miners, in the 48th Pennsylvania Volunteer Regiment. It was decided by the Union command to dig a tunnel under the fortifications, set off a huge explosion, break through the Confederate lines, and thus end the Civil War. This was in July of 1864.

The Pennsylvania miners did dig a tunnel. Right under the Confederate fortifications they placed 8,000 pounds of explosives, and set off the charge. It made such a large crater it exists to this day, and a main street in Petersburg is named for it, Crater Road.

The explosion did what was expected, it blew a huge hole in the Confederate line. The follow-up on the part of the Union forces was disastrous and poorly organized, also slow. The Confederates quickly brought up reinforcements and soon plugged the gap. There was dissension among the Union officers, which was the cause of the bungled attack after the explosion. The miners had done their job to perfection. Had the follow-up been done in a more organized and forceful manner, the Civil War may well have ended at that time. As it was, it went on another ten months. The honor for that event goes to the Union miners who dug the tunnel, and the quick-acting Confederates who plugged it up again.

Sergeant Harry Reese of Shamokin gained distinction in this particular battle. He volunteered to replace a defective fuse which failed to ignite the four tons of high explosives at the end of the tunnel. He entered the tunnel, replaced the fuse, ignited the new one, then returned to safety. Within moments a mammoth explosion took place. Sgt. Reese survived the ensuing battle and returned to Shamokin after the war. He then became the Chief Burgess, which is the highest elected official of a borough. This is equivalent to the mayor of a city.

Sergeant
Harry Reese

60

The Unexpected Use of Dynamite

Many miners were knowledgeable in the use of dynamite. Several times, in my memories of childhood, there
would appear an article in the local paper about an aged
miner who took his life with dynamite. The procedure was
utmost simplicity. The would be suicide would obtain one
or more sticks of dynamite, attach blasting caps to it, attach
a fuse, light the fuse, and walk out into an open place. Place
is not quite the best word, nor are field and plain any more
accurate. Around many breakers are barren and flat, or
almost flat places covered with coal dirt, which is also not
pure coal dirt, but a mixture of fine coal, dust, rock dust,
slate, and other mining detritus. In these areas virtually
nothing grows except the hardiest of weeds. It would be in
such a place, familiar surroundings, in which the miner
would take his last walk. There was no funeral expense.
These people were poor, and money was a consideration.
After the explosion, a finger or toe might be found, but little
else. These gaudy exits drew a paragraph or two in the local
paper, and were considered trifling news indeed. Most of
the local miners were Catholic, and suicide was frowned
upon.

Children living near mines and breakers, and quite a
few of them did, would occasionally break into the storage
buildings and pilfer blasting caps. They would then attempt to burn them, or maybe pound on them with rocks,
with tragic results. A blasting cap can take off a hand or foot
very easily. When a theft of caps occurred, notices were
placed in the papers for parents to question their children
and advise them of the danger.

Shamokin had, and has, a creek running through it
bearing sulphur water from the mines. When the mines are
working, it is black; when they are not, it is a nasty brownish
green. One Halloween some older boys obtained some

dynamite, placed it in a washtub, ignited the fuse, and floated it down the stream. It went off in an open place with a terrific roar. The stream parallels the main street and business section of town, so the explosion caused much uproar and comment. The stream is crossed by several bridges, and the dynamite could as easily gone off under any of them with pedestrians walking about 12 or 13 feet above the water. This prank was not considered funny by anybody, young or old, and was not repeated again.

Fresh water lake and sandy beach at Tuscarora State Park near Mahanoy City, Pennsylvania.

When Pappy Drank the Horse Liniment

Grandpa Bert would sometimes have headaches from the fumes and noise of the dynamite he worked with in the mines. He kept an array of patent medicines on the cellar steps which he would use to alleviate the condition. Among these bottles was a bottle of horse liniment. This was a thick white liquid product used on the mine mules. The mules spent much of their lives in the mines, which were always cool and damp. Subsequently, they became arthritic, and were rubbed with liniment to prolong their usefulness. Pap figured if it was good for the mules it was good for him, and he used it for the same purpose.

One time, while he experienced a throbbing headache, he went to the cellar stairway, which was a dark place, and selected a bottle of horse liniment rather than the intended medicine. He took a deep draught of the stuff, and flew out into the middle of the living room floor, bouncing on the floor, furniture, and walls. Rebecca thought he was having some incredible fit of some kind, in that he was not able to respond to questions. It was 10 minutes or more until he was able to drink some water and tell what happened. To be sure, the horse liniment from that time forward was not kept around the other medications.

Our First Music Job

In the thirties there was no television, and not all homes had radios, either. It seemed that many more children then took music lessons than do now. Girls would take lessons on piano, violin, or flute, the boys took lessons on any instruments. When I was no more than 8, at least six boys in my block took lessons. We were good enough to play in the junior band, so we knew simple marches.

One day a small-time local politician came around to the neighborhood in a pickup truck with signs on it. The signs said to vote for him for something. He asked us if we would play marches all afternoon while he drove us around town. This was to attract attention and get votes for him. He promised us each a quarter. There was a saxophone player (me), a trumpet player, a clarinet player, a trombone player, and something else. We got in the back of the pickup truck and played marches all afternoon. Maybe not real good, but loud. Lots of people came out of their houses and saw the politician's signs.

When we got back to our own block, the politician said we didn't play good enough and it wasn't worth a quarter. I was the youngest and began weeping, the others were angry and argued with him. Just then the father of the clarinet player came around the corner and asked what was wrong. He was a big fellow, very muscular, and he had a bad temper.

When his son told him, he seized the politician and told him to pay up immediately, 50¢ each, or things would go very hard on him instantly. The politician was a small fellow, and saw the wisdom of this action, so he paid us all on the spot.

The miners did rough work, but a lot of them knew and appreciated music. There was one of them, Harry Lincoln, who worked in the Cameron with Pap Chaundy.

64

He (Harry) was a composer of music and he actually had some of his compositions produced and sold as sheet music. My wife had a piece by him in her piano bench, and I remember seeing his name on sheet music when I was a child.

A mine fan at Honesville on the bank of Mahanoy Creek. Remnant of the Lawrence Colliery. The head of a full-grown man would come up to the center axle on this fan. The author's granduncle, Floyd, lost his life working on a fan like this when it was accidentally turned on while he was working.

Photo by Christine Goldbeck of the Shenandoah Evening Herald, Pennsylvania.

The Forgetful Barber

Mr. Green was the barber on Spruce Street. Parents would send their little children to him with a quarter and a note of how they wanted the child's hair cut.

Mr. Green dearly loved to talk about politics and business. In the summer the door stood open and any passerby might stop in a little while to get or give some opinions on these subjects.

Mr. Green knew all of his customers and their children very well. One time a child came in while Mr. Green was engaged in a lively discussion with another old fellow. The child handed him a note and got up in the barber chair. He draped the big colored cloth over the child, laid the note aside, and set to work. There was barely any interruption in his oration of what the country needed in the way of political improvement.

A few minutes later he stepped back to proudly survey his handiwork. It was a style then called a "baldy," very short all over the head, very common for boys in the summertime. He held up a hand mirror for the child to see infront and back, reflected in the wall mirror.

"My Momma's not gonna like that." said the child, mournfully.

"What do you mean, your Momma's not gonna like that? You're a fine looking little boy." Mr. Green was shocked anyone would question his skill.

"No I'm not either. I'm a girl." said the tot, most unhappily.

"What!" cried Mr. Green as he whipped the cloth off her. There she sat, red dress, white anklets, Mary Janes, girl all the way.

"Good Heavens!" exclaimed Mr. Green, as he picked up the note and read it carefully.

"Mr. Green, give my daughter a nice page boy bob for

the summer. Make a nice straight set of bangs, but not too low. Thank you."

The old man who had been engaged in heated political discussion looked on in surprise. He could see Mr. Green was upset by the mistake. He inquired politely, "What are you gonna do about that, George?"

"She'll just have to wear a sunhat for the summer, that's all I can think. Confounded kids in that family all look alike." said Mr. Green, with a trace of annoyance in his voice.

Mr. Green turned to the forlorn little child. "Here's your money back, Jeanie. Next time you come in remind me that you're a girl."

The very unhappy little girl took the money and slowly walked up Spruce Street. My guess is she never came back, and who could blame her?

Mischief with the Dinky Cable Rolls

A colliery was the name given to the entire mining operation at a given site. This would include the mine, breaker, outbuildings, track, cars, engines, and culm dumps. Some of these places originated in the middle 1800's, and after decades of operation, were huge.

The Cameron mine was one of the largest. Its culm dump was said to be the largest in the world. The culm dump was on the side of a good sized mountain, for the area, and went right to the top of the mountain. The mountains of the hard coal region are part of the Appalachian chain, running from New England to Georgia. They are not extremely high, such as the Rockies, but they are mountains all the same, geologically very old.

After the coal was brought up from the mine shaft, it was passed through the breaker which crushed it and separated it into various sizes, rice, pea, stone, egg, run-of-the-mine, and I don't know what all anymore. The slate and rock were separated from the coal, and transported by means of little cable cars, called "dinkies," to the top of the culm dump. Culm dumps were not usually called that. More normally, it was the "column bank." The colloquial speech of the area was a curious blend and mixture of Irish and numerous European inflections, interspersed with some Pennsylvania Dutch constructions.

"Where's your brudder, Mike?" "Up onna column bank wit' Stevie. Dere flyin ner kites." "Let's go find 'em. Wait'll I outen na light inne attic."

The culm dumps, from a distance, appeared to be simply immense piles of coarse gray and blackish gravel. Up close, they were actually composed of some very large stones for the most part, and you climbed up and down them, not walked or ran. Vegetation did not grow on the culm dumps of coarse material, though some seeds might appear on those that contained coal dirt or regular dirt.

The top of the culm dump overlooking Shamokin was called "Windy Point," and was a great place to fly kites. An incredibly crude road wound round the lower reaches of the dump where it extended from the mountain, then wound its way up through the forest sides of the mountain, coming out on top of the mountain and leading to the culm dump.

The Cameron breaker was in a valley at the bottom of the mountain, with the black creek (called crick) flowing past, and railroad tracks for the coal cars. Attached to the breaker was a building with cables and winches to carry the mine waste to the top of the mountain. Two sets of tracks carried the dinky cars from the mine to the top of the culm bank. They did not make a round trip; when one went up, the other came down.

The cables that pulled these dinkies were of woven steel, thick, black and greasy. Mine employees would quickly chase children away from the tracks and cables if they got near them. This was not because the dinkies traveled so fast, they were rather slow. It was because close to the tipple the tracks angled up at a steep pitch, then dropped forward precipitately, causing the dinkies to drop the load of mine waste.

The cables traveled flat along the ground most of the distance from the mine to the tipple, but at the tipple, the cables rose twenty or thirty feet in the air. When the dinky had completed the journey, the winch machinery was turned off momentarily to reverse the cables, and at that time they would become slack and lie on the ground. In a minute or two, when the winch reversed, the cables would tighten in an instant, and fly up in the air. A person attempting to walk over the cable when it tightened up would have been thrown halfway down the mountain. We stayed well away from the cables.

69

Cable spool of the size we rolled down the Cameron culm bank.

Large cable spool above 8 feet high, would require machines to move.

The cables had to be replaced every couple of years. They came on huge wooden spools, maybe 5 or 6 feet in diameter, and very heavy. These spools were large enough ɔ roll down the sides of the culm bank, rough as it was. The ides of the bank were very steep, giving the spools terrific speed in their descent. As they gained speed, they would go into great bouncing leaps, to smash to pieces on the rocks at the bottom of the bank. The top of the culm bank was large enough, and stretched far enough away from the tipple, that children could roll several spools down the bank and get away before the mine workers could catch them.

The spools were worthless, which is why they were discarded on the culm bank, but they were capable of doing much damage if they rolled down the wrong side of the mountain.

One fine beautiful summer day, some playmates and I took our kites to the top of the bank. Lo and behold, two nice spools were right there on the edge. Rolling spools was far more exciting than flying kites, so we immediately decided to roll them down. On the side of the bank farthest from the tipple, there were trees at the bottom, where the bank overlaid the original mountain. We decided to roll the spools into the trees so they would do no harm. The spools were too heavy for one boy to stand up, but two or three of us could get them up all right. We rolled them to the edge, aimed them carefully, and bump, bump, crash, down they went.

As soon as the second spool was disposed of, we all flew down the road off the bank, in that once you did anything with the spools, just playing around them, you would be run off. In the 1930's, in that poor time and place, if you did something wrong, you could be hit or kicked by an adult. If your parents found out, you could be hit or kicked again. Matter of fact, you could be hit by anyone, male or female, who was bigger than you, so the best thing was to get away if you could.

The road wound through the woods at the bottom of the bank. We quickly reached the bottom of the bank and decided to see if we could find the spools and see what they had done to the trees, if anything. When we entered the woods, we found 6 or 7 boys, whom we knew, about our own age, all of them in the topmost branches of the trees. They cursed us lavishly for rolling the spools down where they were playing, though they were not really angry, in that they would have rolled the spools down themselves, if they found them first. They had seen us lining the spools up on the edge of the bank, and knowing what was coming, climbed instantly to the tops of the larger trees while the spools came down at them. The spools were heavy enough to knock over the smaller trees, which they knew, so they were safe if the spools didn't take an unexpected bound and pick them off the top of the trees.

We were glad nobody got hurt, and I lost interest in rolling the spools down the mountain after that.

The Little Girl in Pittston

My wife was from Pittston. When I was little, we heard of the little girl who was walking along the sidewalk when it opened up beneath her, and she was buried alive and killed. This happened on Mill Street in Pittston, 2 blocks from my wife's childhood home.

The story had passed out of my memory, but when my wife and I were newlyweds, and visiting her relatives in Pittston, we drove by the site where the tragedy occurred. My wife pointed out the spot, commenting that it was where the girl fell in when she was a child, about 1937.

In barest essentials, the girl, who was 5 or 6 at the time, and her aunt had gone to a nearby grocery store. They were returning home with their purchases, the aunt walking several paces before the child, who frolicked along merrily behind her. There was a rumble, the ground shook, and the aunt turned around to see a widening hole appearing where the child had been. The surrounding earth continued to collapse into the hole.

Rescue efforts were initiated immediately but it was several days before the child's body could be recovered. As I had done when the boy fell into the Nelson shaft, my wife attended the viewing of the unfortunate tot, who was 2 years younger than she.

The rescue effort gained national publicity, and was attended by a photographer from "Life" magazine and the major news services. The site was restored as it had been before the cave-in, and is undetectable now. I have walked over the spot in the past year. It is located on a narrow street, lined with old wooden individual houses with neat little lawns in front of them. Such a peaceful scene, now, in the summer with pretty flowers blooming in the yards.

This cave-in was not an air hole. In the early days of mining, little thought was given to the future of the earth

A view of the sidewalk in Pittston where the earth opened and swallowed the little girl. Flagstones mark the original sidewalk, before the cave-in. It took several days to get the girl out.

above the mines. Where the veins of coal divided, a large underground room was excavated to switch the dinky cars. If this slope was considered worked out, columns of coal supporting the roof of the tunnel, or underground rooms, were removed when it was decided to terminate mining operations there. Their practice, called "robbing pillars", contributed to the occasional collapse of the earth above. Underground streams could also flow through abandoned mine slopes, removing additional material. The collapse of the earth above these abandoned mine workings could be very extensive.

When my wife was in 8th grade, she expected to attend the nearby school, just a few blocks from her home. That year the gym floor collapsed into a cave-in beneath the school, dropping 200 feet, so claimed the neighbors. People exaggerate. Maybe it was only a hundred feet. Whatever it was, the school was closed immediately, a high wire fence was constructed around it, and so it remains to this time. In appearance, the school is very substantial, of brick construction, and gives no external evidence of the damage within. The walls are not cracked, the windows intact. One might think it was still in use. It may never be used again.

A mine cave-in affecting the yard of a home on Fulton Street in Pittston, Pennsylvania, about 1944. What looks like a small bush is the top of a tree sticking up out of the hole in the ground. The tree is the same size as those in the background. The girls, Florence, Rosalie, and Christina, were returning home from choir practice at the Lithuanian Church. The small picture is of Florence at around that time.

The high school in Pittston where the gym dropped. No injuries resulted from this mishap.

Backyard Bootleg Holes

During the depression years many miners were out of work. Money was hard to come by, and the families re-sorted to many expedients to survive. One of the methods was that of stealing coal. Perhaps "stealing" is too harsh a word, for an activity that wasn't very seriously frowned upon. Stealing coal was sort of like stealing some ears of corn out of the cornfield. It wasn't right, but it wasn't any big deal, either.

Coal was stolen in various ways. Young boys would climb up on the top of loaded coal cars on the railroad while the train was moving slowly, then throw the coal off on the ground along the tracks. Later they would come by with baskets and burlap sacks to gather up the coal. Older ladies would take their baskets near the mines and pluck out good pieces of coal from the culm dumps, or what fell off the trucks on bumpy roads.

The economic scale of these ventures was very modest indeed. When coal sold for $6.00 a ton, a hundred pounds represented 30 cents. However, if you had no money at all, a savings of thirty cents was certainly worth while. In those days, there were still railroad police on the trains. While I never knew it to happen, it was possible that someone could be arrested for stealing coal in that fashion.

Young men who had their own dump trucks were more venturesome in their efforts to steal a truckload of coal. They would drive to the small breakers in the middle of the night, and load up as quickly as possible. Even the small breakers had night watchmen sometimes to prevent that sort of thing, and the culprits were not only subject to arrest, but had to endure the hazard of being fired upon with shotguns carried by the watchmen.

The mine towns were naturally built close to where the coal was found. Houses could be located close to where

78

View of a typical abandoned bootleg hole in the anthra-cite region. These were good places to avoid entering. The wood shoring would rot over the years, permitting the roof to cave in.

coal seams came to the surface. At times, unemployed miners would embark on their own independent ventures, mining coal near their homes, or at times in their own back yards. These operations were invariably more dangerous than the regular mines, in that the miners did not want to disturb the neighbors enough to make them complain about what was going on. For this reason, larger pieces of equipment, such as fans for the air shafts were not employed. Sheer poverty also contributed to the lack of safety equipment.

These mines were often small family endeavors. When I was in high school, one of our classmates worked in a mine in his own back yard, along with his father and several brothers. During the senior year, the mine collapsed, killing the father and seriously injuring the brothers. I would guess there are still a few bootleg holes in operation, no matter the danger involved.

Carbide and Canaries

Carbide is a light powdery chemical that, when mixed with water, forms a gas called acetylene. This gas burns with a bright white flame. Miners had small brass lamps which were affixed to their caps, using carbide gas as an illuminant. The bottom section of the lamp could be unscrewed. In this was placed the carbide, than a small amount of water was added. There was a little arm-like lever to adjust the flow of gas, and thereby, the length of the flame. It was a nice handy little light, except that the open flame would ignite an unsuspected pocket of gas once in a while, with fatal consequences to those in the vicinity.

To attempt to avoid such calamities, the early miners carried canaries in cages into the mines. The birds chirped away as cheerfully as on the surface. They had the good quality of being very sensitive to small quantities of gas that might be present. If the bird stopped singing, danger may be present. If the bird fell off its perch, leave immediately.

The timber used for shoring up the ceiling of the mine tunnel creaked and groaned their own messages of safety or danger. The miners were very adept at distinguishing normal contraction or shifting sounds from those indicating possibly dangerous strains or overload.

It was in this area of safety, or lack of it, that bootleg miners often came to grief. They used most any old wood at hand for timbering, and this in insufficient quantity. A bootleg hole was not a forgiving work place. Errors lived on in the memories of the surviving friends and relatives. Even in the present, with modern safety devices, government agencies to inspect them, and strong unions to insist upon their use, mining is one of the more hazardous occupations.

The main air shaft into the McDade Park mine. The top is closed and a powerful fan forced air down the shaft into the mine. If needed, the canister pictured could be lowered down the shaft to bring up workers in the event of a malfunction of the dinky car hoist. The dinky cars went down the main slope into the mine. This equipment is kept in good operating condition.

This is the bottom of the shaft, almost 300 feet down. The air is cold and damp, there is a lot of water in mines. There was a ditch beside the tracks when mules were used, the mule walked between the tracks, the driver walked in the ditch.

The mine tipple at McDade Park in Scranton. Dump trucks drove underneath of it to be loaded with coal. It did not have the sign "tipple" on it when it was a working mine. If someone didn't know what it was, better not to be around it.

A mine car fitted with seats to carry the miners down the main slope into the mine, about a quarter mile, and about 300 feet below the surface. It was considered a significant concession to comfort that the seat boards were installed tilted. The miners could sit straight on the journey. A mine car of this size fully loaded would hold 5 tons of coal.

How Polish Girls Sang "Silent Night"

Miners worked hard, played hard, and died hard. The saloon was, and is an omnipresent feature of neighborhood life. My great grandfather was a musician, my grandfather was a musician, my father was a musician, and I was a musician. When I was 13 I began playing in the saloons of the coal regions.

In the family, it was not thought unusual to be a musician, it was more like a naturally expected thing. This was for the men, the women were a little different. None of them seemed to play piano good enough for church, much less the saloon, but they all seemed to have had enough lessons to know whether or not a child was practicing his lesson right.

The small towns of the coal regions have numerous saloons. I once heard that Girardville, where Kehoe's place was, had more saloons per capita (1 for every 60 people) than anywhere else in the United States. This statement is not offered as fact, nor have I any interest in researching the matter. There were, and are, a lot of them. Curiously, a lot of them had "hotel" as part of their name, but were in no sense whatever a hotel where you could obtain lodging. When I played in the places, years ago, hotel was the most commonly used term by which to call them, rather than saloon, bar, lounge, or whatever.

Around the Christmas holidays, jobs were easy to find, as almost every little place had a couple of musicians. There was The Slovak Club, The Lithuanian Club, The Polish Club, The Italian Club, and other ethnic places. It seemed that at least once every Christmas season, at The Polish Club, or whatever Club, there would be a pretty young girl who wanted to sing "Silent Night" in her native language. This would come toward the end of the evening, after much encouragement from her father, uncles, or brothers, who were miners and coal truck drivers. The male relatives of these girls always seemed well over 6 feet tall and strong as bulls.

The girl was timid so she would start too high. When she reached the higher notes of the song, she couldn't make them, and would falter and stop. Glares at the band from the assembled relatives. She would try again, this time too low. More glares and muttered curses at the band from the relatives. She would give it one last try. Happy day, she got it right, and at the end much clapping and good wishes from the friends, and relatives, with drinks being sent around to friends, relatives, and the band.

It is important to realize that the girl really could sing the song very well. This is why she was encouraged to do it in the first place. The girls were very pretty, and made a charming scene as they sang "Silent Night," or other songs, in their family language. My own wife still speaks Lithuanian to her mother, as do all the older sisters.

Thomas Edison and St. Edward's Church

Grandpa Eddie belonged to St. Edward's Church. It was an old church, one of the earliest in town. In the early mining towns, many of the homes and business buildings were of plain, or even crude construction, the churches were as nicely made as the people could afford. St. Edward's had a claim to distinction, in that it was the very first church ever to be illuminated with electric lights, installed personally by Thomas Edison around 1880, more or less.

Other than St. Edward's Church, the only other claims of note about Shamokin was that the culm bank was supposed to be the largest in the world, and that one of the slopes in the Cameron extended seven miles from the main shaft to the workface. This was reputed to be the longest in the world, leading underground out past a very small town called Trevorton. Shamokin is the southern end of the anthracite fields, once away from Shamokin in that direction lies farmland and the Amish.

These facts, if they are facts, or items of local interest if they are not facts, have never appeared in any book of records that I have seen. Whether or not, they were of interest to the residents of the community.

In the 30's, the miners rode to the workface on dinky cars outfitted with crude bench seats, the cars pulled by low electric engines. As children, we would hang over the entrance to the mine as the dinkies went in, and wave to the miners. Their faces were clean, and you could recognize someone you knew. If you shouted and waved, someone might wave back at you. When the miners had completed the shift, if you hung over and waved, no one even looked up at you, and you would not have recognized your own brother for the coal dirt. No one looked up at you, because everyone was exhausted. Mine labor was unremitting toil, sufficient to tax the strongest.

St. Edward's Church, beautiful historical St. Edward's Church, was made of wood, as were most buildings in the town. A few years back it burned to the ground. Maybe now no one knows or cares that Thomas Edison put electric lights in it. It has since been rebuilt just as it was.

Franklin B. Gowen

Franklin Benjamin Gowen got his start in Shamokin. He married a girl from Sunbury, came up to Shamokin, and set up a mine at Brady. Brady is a little village just outside of Shamokin. Gowen's Dad gave him the money to start the mine, the venture was unsuccessful and he went broke. Gowen wrote the first union contract ever written with the miners, maybe it was the first union contract in industry. He should have remembered this when he got rich and famous.

Gowen left Shamokin, went to Pottsville, and "read law" for six years. His Dad assisted him again. By a stroke of luck, he became the head of the Reading Coal and Iron Company by his late 30's. It was like going from unemployed to the president of General Motors in 8 years. The Reading was the largest commercial enterprise in the United States at the time. Gowen was as famous at that time as Astor, Vanderbilt, Rockefeller, or any other great name in American business or industry.

If Gowen had been more fair with the miners, there'd probably be statues of him all over the coal regions. As it was, his ambition ran away with him, and he plunged the Reading into debt and bankruptcy. A few years later he took his own life in Washington, D.C. at the age of 49. All very sad.

The Handprint on the Jail Wall

As a child, I heard a story, more like a legend, about some miner who was hanged who claimed to be innocent. He placed his hand, grimy with coal dust, on the wall of the jail cell where he was imprisoned. It left a hand print on the wall, which he said would prove his innocence. He stated that the print would remain as long as the jail stood. The print has remained to this day, despite all attempts to remove it.

The above account is basically the bare bones of the story. The time was about 1877, the location at Mauch Chunk, Pennsylvania. Indian names abound in Pennsylvania, and Mauch Chunk is one of them. Mauch Chunk was not a village populated with real Indians such as might be found in the Southwestern part of the country, but curiously enough, it was renamed Jim Thorpe, to honor the great Indian athlete who is buried there. Jim Thorpe is the name of the place now.

It was called Mauch Chunk when Alec Campbell was hanged there, and I will use that name in this recitation. Alec Campbell was accused of shooting and killing a mine superintendent named Morgan Powell. Another Mollie named "Yellow Jack" Donohue admitted to the shooting, and was hanged also for the same crime.

Mauch Chunk is a pretty little town, situated in a deep valley between coal-bearing mountains, with a stream and railroad tracks running through it, an arrangement typical of many small coal towns. A long, winding, narrow street leads upward out of town, to the top of one of the mountains. On this street is the jail, appearing today as it did in 1877. It is not of the awesome ugliness of the jail in Pottsville, but it is not the local beauty spot, either, by a long sight.

When visiting the coal region last summer, I went to Girardville, where there is a saloon known as Jack Kehoe's

Mauch Chunk Jail, Pennsylvania. Almost the same as a century ago. It is in cell 17 that the handprint is located. A guest register that was kept for many years showed that many famous and prominent people took the trouble to visit the place. The author's great grandpa John was in the same jail at the same time as Alec Campbell, also on Molly charges. Great Grandpa got 3 1/2 years for his activities.

The handprint is located high up on the wall on the right side. The wall curves into the ceiling. This cell is still in regular use.

Note: Since the above picture was taken, a new jail has been constructed. This building is now in private ownership.

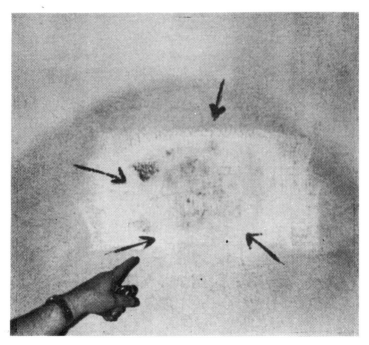

The handprint of Alec Campbell on the wall of cell
number 17. He said it would last as long as the jail stood.

Hibernian House. This enterprise is operated by a lady named Alice Wayne, granddaughter of Jack Kehoe. As noted in the earlier section on the Mollies, this kind and gracious lady had much information on the local history. I inquired of her about the hand print on the jail wall, and was assured by her that it could still be seen.

Alec Campbell was brought to the jail, as the story went that I heard in childhood. He did place his grimy left hand on the wall, leaving a mark. He must have been a good-sized lad, in that I am of average size, and had to reach up straight to place my hand where the print remained. I had gone to the jail at Mauch Chunk, and received permission from Sheriff Hoherchak to inspect the cell, number 17. The public was once permitted to stream through, but the jail is in continuous use, and it became a burden on the officials. The hand print placed on the wall more than a century ago, is plain to be seen. The wall had been re-painted, replastered, re-everything, and the print still comes back. The cell is small, with a vaulted ceiling, tiny window, and massive iron door. While there, I pondered briefly how many miserable social misfits had occupied this gloomy place since Alex placed his hand on the wall. Quite a few, to be sure.

At the railroad station in Mauch Chunk there is a little gift and souvenir shop. I purchased there a booklet concerning the activities of the Mollies. It gives the same view, which is that of the mine owners, as is presented in Doyle's "Valley of Fear." Even as biased as this little tract is, and it certainly is, there emerges a picture of the miners' working conditions. A sixty hour week of brutal toil was the norm, paid at the rate of about 50 cents per day. When the miner made his few paltry purchases at the end of the week at the company store, he owed more than he made. This is the same miner described by Doyle as "well-paid, with good working conditions." Good working conditions, as described by my Grandpa Bert, was to take a canary into the mine. When the bird stopped singing, you prepared to leave. If it fell off its perch, you left as quick as you could, if your carbide lamp didn't explode the methane gas before you could get out.

The pamphlet ends on a triumphant note with the hanging of Jack Kehoe and 21 other miners. Since the pamphlet was published, Jack Kehoe was granted a posthumous full pardon by the governor of Pennsylvania, and exonerated of the crime of which he was convicted.

The story of the Mollies is a complex and fascinating point in American history. Many factors were involved. British capital developed the anthracite mines. Irish laborers, who had left Ireland in the potato famine of 1848, provided a ready source of workers. Political animosities were brought to the new land, as well as religious ones. The wealthy mine owners were Protestant, the Irish miners Catholic. It was a time in American history described as a period of labor strife, with the first attempts at the formation of unions in the coal, steel, and railroad industries. In western Pennsylvania, the oil industry was in a period of astounding growth, in turn feeding money into the steel industry of Pittsburgh. People of unbelievable wealth built palaces in Newport, to be attended by servants receiving two dollars a week. Civil War veterans, North and South, in pain from their wounds, purchased laudanum and morphine at the neighborhood grocery store, while new lands were opened in the west.

Alec Campbell lost his unfortunate life in a colorful and fascinating era. Whether he was innocent or not of the crime for which he died, only God knows, this century later. The hand print remains, a silent and eerie reminder of the miners of that long-gone time.

Alec Campbell, famed for the handprint
on the Mauch Chunk jail wall.

Patrick Campbell, the great grand-nephew of Alec, de-
voted 15 years of his life to intensive research in an effort to
make a final decision as to the guilt or innocence of Alec. The
effort was disappointing. By contemporary standards, Alec
would not have been convicted, but it was impossible to obtain
solid and indisputable evidence as to Alec's guilt or innocence.

Despite this, Patrick had a success beyond imagining in
the new information he brought to light in his book, "A Molly
Maguire Story." This information should result in a long over-
due re-appraisal of this period of American Labor history, and
add a new perspective on the Molly Maguire trials.

Daddy Longlegs in the Coffee Grinder

Children can be mischievous and adults don't know half so much as they think they do sometimes. We had an old fashioned coffee grinder in the cellar fastened up on a pole by the coal bin. It was a red box-like contraption with a little hinged lid on top through which coffee beans could be poured into it. There was a small glass window on the front so you could see how many coffee beans were in it. On the right side was a hand crank you turned to grind up the coffee beans. Last of all, there was a little platform underneath to place a cup or whatever to collect the ground coffee.

Cellars of those houses were crude affairs, dug out of the dirt, maybe a concrete slab for the coal bin part, and rough stone walls. It was easy for bugs and mice to come in. In the summer and fall of the year there was a kind of spider that came around which we called daddy longlegs. It has a little body about as big as a pea, and long skinny legs like stiff threads, they would be maybe two or three inches in size. They were harmless, couldn't bite, and it was easy to pick them up by their long thin legs.

One day when several children were playing in the cellar we noticed a daddy longlegs in the grinder looking out the window at us. We turned the crank and he came out just like a coffee bean, teeny bits. There was no television in those days, and next to no money for amusements, either. But there were lots of daddy longlegs. We would collect throngs of them, drop them in the top, and when there was a bunch of them in the window, crank away. They didn't look too different from coffee when they came out on the platform, and the grown-ups didn't seem to notice any least difference when they used the coffee machine.

Children were not permitted to have coffee at that time. An equitable arrangement. We children did not get any coffee, the grown-ups did not have any fun converting the daddy longlegs to percolator size.

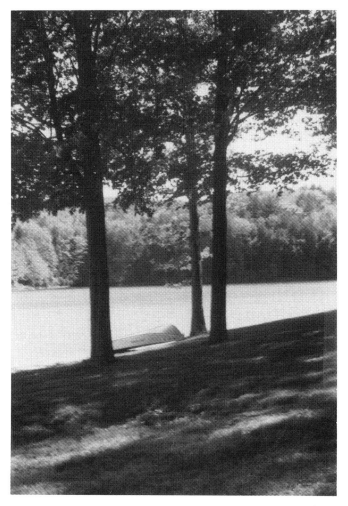

Idyllic scene by the lake at Tuscarora State Park near Mahanoy City, Pennsylvania.

APPENDIX

Epilogue

In this small work I have tried to address three themes of importance. The first and most obvious is that of the everyday life of the miner and his family. The second is the dreadful labor strife of that period between the end of the Civil War and the turn of the century. The last theme is to try to relate the importance of coal to the development of other major American industries, particularly steel, railroads, oil, and the electric utilities. It would be overstating the case to insist that coal was the base and energy source of all American industry. It is not overstating the case at all to hold that coal was a very important factor and influence on the subsequent major industries that followed.

Shortly after 1800 the canals of the United States became of huge importance in the transport of bulk materials and foodstuffs. The canal boat was slow but marvelously economical. A mule could pull a canal boat loaded with a hundred tons of coal at four miles an hour. A hundred tons is about as much as is contained in a modern full-size railroad hopper car, which is quite a lot. The very earliest railroads were of a short distance, to carry coal from the mine to the canal boat.

The canal boat era almost leaped into prominence around 1830, and by 1842 reached such overwhelming importance in Pennsylvania that the state came very close to going bankrupt building canals. After the Civil War the railroads forged ahead as bulk carriers, displacing the canal boats and companies, and by the turn of the century the colorful canal boat era had come and gone. The memory lingers on in the names of many Pennsylvania communities ending in "port" or "haven." Some railroads turned into canal companies, some canal companies became railroads, some companies operated both almost from the beginning.

Around 1840, the iron manufacturers along the

Susquehanna River near Harrisburg discovered that anthracite coal could be used, rather than charcoal, to smelt iron ore. In a few years, what had been little more than family businesses grew to be gigantic enterprises at Steelton, Columbia, and Safe Harbor. Coal to fuel this enterprise was brought down the Susquehanna by canal boat, and the original canal can still be seen to this day at Steelton. Bituminous coal was also put to use very early on, and was used to develop the steel mills of Pittsburgh and other cities. The Schuylkill and Lehigh Rivers brought coal to fuel the industries along their courses, with Bethlehem and Allentown growing into major manufacturing centers. The Delaware and Hudson canal took coal to the New York market, the Schuylkill took it to Philadelphia, The Susquehanna took it to Baltimore via the Chesapeake Bay.

Oil was discovered in northwestern Pennsylvania in 1858 by Colonel Drake at Titus Creek. The very first oil shipments were on wooden rafts floated downriver to Pittsburgh on spring freshets. The rafts would sometimes get smashed on rocks, with a loss of life and the oil cargo all together. Soon after, in the 1860's, the oil was transported by flatcar in monstrous wooden barrels. These flatcars were pulled by steam powered locomotives burning coal. The diesel powered locomotives did not come into widespread use until after World War I.

The earliest electrical utilities used direct current developed by generators that were powered by steam engines. Street lights were installed at Sunbury, Pennsylvania in 1882, with Thomas Edison supervising the work. He then came to Shamokin and installed them there, also putting electric lights in St. Edward's Roman Catholic Church. The direct current form of electricity was superseded a decade later by the alternating current invented by Nikola Tesla, which then became the standard of the world. The electric generating stations became gigantic markets for anthracite (hard) and bituminous (soft) coal.

The labor strife in Pennsylvania reached a peak with the Molly Maguire trials, and public sentiment was so antagonistic towards miners unions, and unions in general, that the growth of unions was severely impeded for two decades, from 1880 to 1900. New evidence coming to light a century later is changing the historical record of the labor relations of that period. Jack Kehoe was posthumously exonerated almost a century later. At a mock trial held to commemorate the hundredth anniversary of the Carbon County Bar Association in December, 1993, Alec Campbell was found to be not guilty by contemporary judicial standards. This trial was arranged by Judge John Lavelle, and it was held in the very same court room in which Alec Campbell was originally tried. Legal steps are under way at this time to exonerate Alec Campbell also.

In a related development, Genia Miller wrote a play entitled "Spirit of the Molly Maguires," which examined the effects of the trial on the families of the accused miners. This play has received a warm welcome in the coal regions.

We review in "Tales" a complex and exciting period of American history. It was real people, their hopes and dreams, successes and failures, loves and hates. It was the life of the ancestors of us who grew up in the coal regions, whether descended from miners or owners, or the others of that time and place. The mines and steel mills created markets for the timber merchants of Williamsport and the shoofly pies of Lancaster, as well as providing business to the bankers of Philadelphia and the famous Philadelphia lawyers. It was, and is, a fascinating era of American history.

The Anthracite Era
(a brief overview)

* Pennsylvania has the richest deposits of anthracite (hard) coal in the United States. This coal has the most carbon in it.

* In 1769 the city of Wilkes-Barre was only a settlement. A local blacksmith named Obadiah Gore had begun using anthracite coal in his forge.

* Coal was found near Mauch Chunk, now Jim Thorpe, in 1781. Colonel Jacob Weiss and others formed the first coal company in the United States, the "Lehigh Coal Mining Company."

* Necho Allen, a hunter from Pottsville, discovered coal in that area in 1790. In the same year Isaac Tomlinson discovered coal at Shamokin. The last important discovery of coal was at Hazleton by another hunter, John Charles, in 1826.

* Around 1840 the iron smelters around Harrisburg found that coal could be used to smelt iron. This led to a huge growth in the construction of canals in Pennsylvania and a corresponding growth in the iron and steel industry. The canal at Steelton, near Harrisburg, is the original one and can be seen to the present time.

* John Siney led a strike at the Eagle Colliery at St. Clair in 1867. The strike was to protest the reduction of pay from 2-1/2 cents per bushel to 2 cents per bushel of coal mined. A strong man could produce 50 bushels in a 15 hour work day using a pick and shovel. The strike was successful and the Workingmen's Benevolent Association was formed.

* The worst early coal mining disaster occurred at the Avondale mine at Plymouth, near Wilkes-Barre. This calamity took place on September 6, 1869, and resulted in the loss of 110 lives, including boys as young as 12. The immediate result of the tragedy was the enactment of laws forbidding the construction of the breaker directly over the mine shaft. The breaker at Avondale caught fire, suffocating all those who were working below ground level. Most of those who perished were Welsh immigrants, and a historic marker has been placed at the site by the National Welsh-American Foundation.

104

Note: The first name for the coal breaker was "coal cracker", the phrase still in use at the time of the Avondale tragedy. "Coal cracker" became a phrase used subsequently to apply to any inhabitant of the anthracite region, not always to the pleasure of the inhabitants.

* In 1873 the Miners National Association was formed. Another organization, the Knights of Labor, was also formed. This group was led by Terence V. Powderly. At a national convention in 1890 the various groups combined as the United Mine Workers of America.

* Mother Jones (Mary Harris Jones), the fearless and controversial organizer of union workers, visited in Coaldale, near Hazleton, in 1900 to assist in organizing the workers of that region into a union.

* Mining was, and is, a dangerous occupation. The peak year for fatalities was 1907, with 708 lives lost in the anthracite region alone. Employment grew in the coal region to 1914, when over 180,000 miners were at work. The production of coal increased to a peak in 1917, when 90 million tons were produced.

* The history of anthracite mining is a history of frequent labor turbulence. In 1925, "The Long Strike" lasted for 170 days. Mines began to close down gradually from that time forward, resulting in a continuous decline in anthracite mining.

* The Knox Mine Disaster in 1958 brought about a huge reduction in coal mining. This was the result of the flooding of the large Northern Coal Field as the Susquehanna River entered the mine at Port Griffith.

* The use of oil as an energy source for diesel engines and gasoline for the automobile, along with the development of air transport, were all factors in diminishing the need for coal as a fuel. The use of gas and oil burning furnaces for home heating resulted in another loss of a market for coal. Vast coal deposits still remain in the United States, and it would be premature to discount coal as an energy source in the future.

All Mining Towns Are Not Alike

Mining, reduced to barest essentials, is the activity of digging a hole in the ground to obtain a desired metal or mineral. The conditions, circumstances, and social organization under which the activity occurs varies as much as any other human activity.

The anthracite region towns and villages were totally different from the gold and silver mining communities of the American West. Hard coal mining took place in settled, established communities with existing customs and social institutions in place. The colliery, with accompanying mining village owned by the mine operator, company store and police force, was a tightly organized and controlled environment. These mining villages grew in near proximity to established farming villages and communities with traditional and conservative social values. Apart from labor strife, these communities were very stable places, and long-lasting. Some of the larger collieries were in operation over a century.

The gold and silver mining towns of the west were very different indeed. The cliche model of bonanza, boardinghouse, bar and bordello was far removed from the company mining village of Pennsylvania. In the west, each miner was out to make his fortune, and he carried a firearm to fight off the Indian or claim-jumper. The prospector went into a wilderness, alone or in small groups, in search of ore deposits. If he found such deposits, a village might spring into existence almost overnight. Each community organized itself in whatever best fashion it could, and some of them were very rough. Stability and longevity were not hallmarks of these communities, and the west is dotted with many ghost towns which were once and briefly centers of bustling activity.

The California gold rush of 1849, the harsh and deadly

Yukon gold rush a few decades later, and the gold and silver rushes to Colorado, Nevada, and Idaho resulted in boom towns. There was but one parallel in Pennsylvania, and that one involved oil, not coal. Pithole, near Oil City, lasted 535 days from beginning to end 1858 to 1859. At the height of the boom, the U.S. Post office at Pithole was the second busiest in the state, exceeded only by Philadelphia. The town boasted a restaurant to rival any on the East Coast. What had once been a scene of frenzied activity is now a lovely pastoral valley, and one must search hard to find the former location of any of the buildings that had been there.

The hard coal mining towns of Pennsylvania were so distinctive that even today there is a noticeable quality about them, as compared with nearby farming or general business communities. Sunbury and Bloomsburg are but a few miles from Shamokin and Mt. Carmel, but there is a difference in appearance of the communities and in the speech patterns (accents) of the residents. This has changed over the decades, but it is still apparent.

Canals for Coal

Few people today realize the importance of canals in the early days of coal mining, or even for general bulk transport. The history of canals as a factor in the development of commerce in the United States is a fascinating study, but it is not the focus of this work. By 1830, canals were in regular use along the Schuylkill River to transport coal to Philadelphia. In the next decade, numerous other canals were built. It was a period described as "canal fever." There was a canal along the Susquehanna River from Harrisburg to Pittston, Pennsylvania. As of this time (1830), 1400 miles of canals were built or under construction, many of them directly related to the coal industry.

By 1830, canals were in regular use along the Schuylkill River to transport coal to the Philadelphia market. The coal boats which went down the Susquehanna ultimately arrived at Port Deposit in Maryland, where the Susquehanna enters the Chesapeake Bay. The coal which was taken to Port Deposit was carried in crude flat boats at first, little more than crude rafts. The next carriers were called "arks", which were somewhat more carefully made, though they were a one-trip item, and they were taken apart at Port Deposit, with both the coal and the lumber being then shipped to the Baltimore market.

Oddly enough, the earliest railroads were very short lines, to carry the coal from the mine to the nearest canal. The Mauch Chunk Railroad was one of this kind, carrying coal from Mauch Chunk (Indian for Bear Mountain) to the Lehigh Coal and Navigation Company about 1818, a distance of 9 miles. Railroads and canals grew together, sometimes they were owned by the same company. The Schuylkill Canal became the property of the Philadelphia and Reading Railroad, which by about 1875 had become the Philadelphia and Reading Coal and Iron Company, the largest industry of the time in the United States. This is the company of which Franklin Gowen was president, "The Ruler of the Reading" is a biography about him.

The process of development of canals continued from 1830 to the time of the Civil War (1861 to 1865), after which railroads saw a period of vast development, with canal transport experiencing a decline. By the turn of the century the canal era had come and gone in the United States.

Canal transport was slow, but marvelously economical. Two mules could pull 3 barges, each loaded with a hundred tons of coal. To give an idea of how much this is, a modern railroad hopper car fully loaded holds about a hundred tons.

COMMEMORATIVE ADDRESS

To the Pennsylvania Labor History Society, October 5, 1974.

This address was given by Mr. John M. Powderly, of the Education Department of the United Steelworkers of America. Mr. Powderly is the grandson of Terence Powderly, first Grand Master Workman of the Knights of Labor, a very early union. The address was a tribute to John Siney, the founder of the Miners and Laborers Benevolent Association at St. Clair, Pennsylvania in 1867.

This address sets forth the hardships of the life of the miner. It is based on a theme in the poem, "And Death Shall Have No Dominion," by Dylan Thomas. The line, "and made them men before they could be boys" holds a poignant significance for me; both of my grandfathers were breaker boys, working full time from the age of 8 or 9.

* *

AND DEATH SHALL HAVE NO DOMINION!

We do not come, John Siney, in widow's weeds, with woeful wailing, summoned by the terrifying scream of the siren signifying death by fire damp, cave-in and hung shot. There has been enough of that... too much of that.

Mammouth, Harwick, Monongah No. 6 and 8, Farmington... Death and the devil dance to the siren's blast... mothers and children chill in the expectation of the roll call. Names called, and some will never answer, and some will never answer. Jacob's Creek, Mather, Orient No. 2, Robena No. 3, Centralia...

AND DEATH SHALL HAVE NO DOMINION!

There are names that will not be mentioned here, John Siney, because they stole the children's childhood and bent them down, and choked them down, and made them men before they could be boys. And when they rose in vengeance for their due, they shot them down. They hanged them down. Lattimer, Mauch Chunk, Harlan County, Ludlow...

AND DEATH SHALL HAVE NO DOMINION!

They owned these dark satanic hills, John Siney, and its precious coal below... they owned the shanty homes scattered in the patch and they owned the scrip and the store. They owned the mules and their traces, and the cops and the courts... and in their arrogance they felt they owned the miner too. There is only one place they can never call their own, John Siney... and we are here, and we are here...Resurrection, Mt. Olive, St. Mary's...

AND DEATH SHALL HAVE NO DOMINION!

Do you know what you have done, John Siney, do you know what you have done? Will my son know what you have done, John Siney, will my son know what you have done? When on the September day on that desolate hillside at Avondale you bore witness to that awful tragedy of ignorance, indifference, thoughtlessness and greed, the travail of ages struggling for expression on your stern, pale face. Did you know, John Siney, when you said, "You can do nothing to win these dead back to life, but you can help me to win fair treatment and justice for the living men who risk life and health in their daily toil", that your words, sanctified by their lives and grim deaths, would strike the chains of millions and lift us up, and lift us up.

Memory is the one true basis of authority, so; Haunt us, John Siney, until these tales be told; Then rest you, Brother Workman, and be warm.

* *

Editorial note: While I agree with the sentiments conveyed in Mr. Powderly's address, I do not regard the hills of my childhood as dark and satanic. The evil deeds of greedy, selfish men were quite apart from the landscape. The mountains of the coal regions were beautiful to me in my childhood and they are beautiful to me in my old age.

112

ANTHRACITE COAL EMPLOYMENT

There was a steady growth of employment in the coal fields after 1850. Following the Civil War, there were various efforts to form unions or other organizations (Knights of Labor) to seek better working conditions in the mines. This movement was almost brought to a halt by the Molly Maguire trials in the late 1870's. In the time period between 1880 and 1900, new waves of immigrants arrived, Slavs, Poles, Hungarians, Ukranians and Italians, to work in the mines. Safety signs in the mines were printed in eight languages. It is customary to speak of all workers in the mines as "miners." In fact, most of the workers were laborers. To become a miner, the worker had to obtain "miners papers," which required training and the ability to read and write. With young boys becoming breaker boys at the age of eight this left little time to acquire any education, and many were almost illiterate. The figures in the graph on the next page are as given, 100,000 is just that. The peak year for employment was 1914, with 180,899 workers employed.

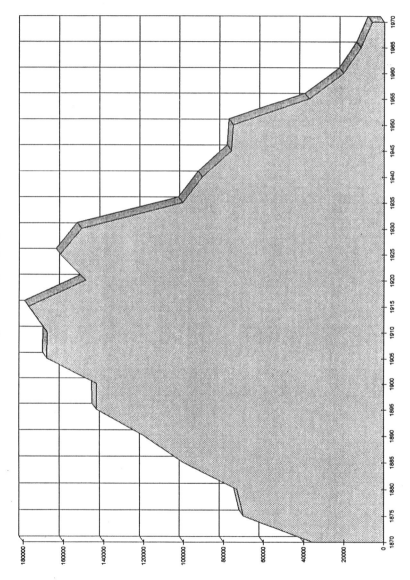

Century of Mining Employment

ANTHRACITE COAL PRODUCTION

Coal mining is a labor-intensive occupation. The first large group of mine workers were those who came to the United States as a result of the Irish Potato Famine of 1848. There was an abundance of coal and a need for it to fuel the industrial growth of the nation. The coal mines were capable of absorbing huge groups of unskilled workers and they did it for several decades. Railroads made possible the transportation of vast amounts of coal, the electric utility and steel industries, along with home heating, created a huge market for coal. The graph on the next page covers the time period from 1870 to 1970. The figures on the left side of the graph are in thousands of tons; 10,000 is ten million, 90,000 is ninety million, and so on. The peak year for production was 1917, with over 89 million tons mined. The source of all data in these graphs is the Pennsylvania Department of Environmental Resources. In the decades following World War I the use of oil and gasoline for fuel reduced the need for coal.

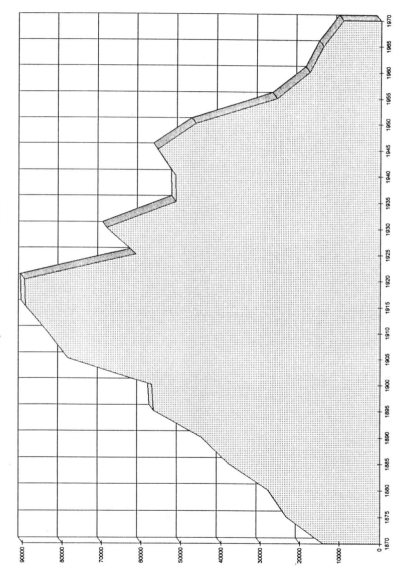

Century of Anthracite Production

ANTHRACITE COAL MINING FATALITIES

Deep coal mining (as contrasted with surface, or strip mining) was among the most dangerous of occupations. Thirty-five thousand miners perished in the anthracite region in the first century of mining, with millions of injuries. The struggle of the miners was always for improved safety measures as well as better wages. The hostility and callousness of the mine operators of that period was incomprehensible. George F. Baer, who followed after Franklin Gowen as a major spokesman for the mine operators, once answered a reporters' question about starving miners with the comment, "They don't suffer. They can't even speak English." This was around the turn of the century. Not surprising with this attitude, mine fatalities peaked in 1907, with 708 miners killed in the anthracite region. The figures in the graph are as given, between 1870 and 1970.

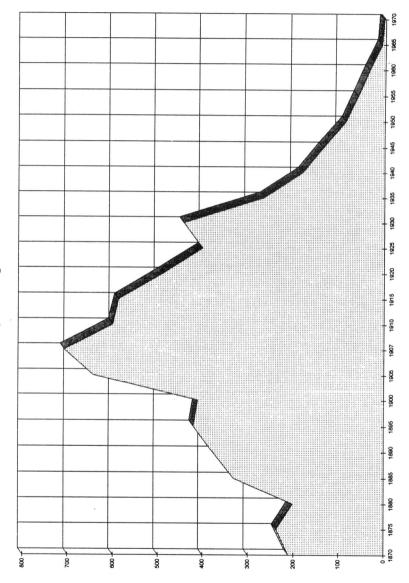

117

Recommended Reading

1. "When Coal Was King," a fascinating publication by Louis Poliniak with numerous photographs of the early days of anthracite coal mining. Nostalgia to those who grew up in the coal regions, quite possibly shocking to those who did not. Applied Arts Publishers, Box 479, Lebanon, PA 17042.

2. "The Mollies Were Men," by Thomas Barrett. The first publication (1969) to attempt to give a balanced presentation of the Molly Maguire trials of a century ago. Most material available on the trials was uniformly condemning of the Mollies from the mine owners' viewpoint. This fed into a lengthy public wave of anti-Irish sentiment, a very insensitive and unfair prejudice. Labor publications about the Mollies were almost as bad the other way, depicting all of them as idealistic and innocent labor martyrs. Some of them were, some of them were not. The true history of the Mollies is a tangled and complex story, still not completely understood.

3. "A Molly Maguire Story," by Patrick Campbell. The great grandnephew of Alec Campbell has spent many years in exhaustive research on the Molly Maguire trials, particularly as they concerned his ancestor. The author has brought to light startling and appalling new information about the mine owners and their associates. This may well result in an extensive revision of the traditional view of this period of American labor history, and well it should. Published by P.H. Campbell, 82 Bentley Avenue, Jersey City, NJ 07304.

4. "Struggle and Lose, Struggle and Win (The United Mine Workers)," by Elizabeth Levy and Tad Richards. Four Winds Press, Division of Scholastic Magazines, Inc., New York, 1977, 122 pages hardcover, $6.95. This is an excellent and easily readable account of the history and development of the United Mine Workers union. Authors Levy and Richards give a straightforward narrative, telling the bad with the good. Of particular interest is the unusually fair presentation of the role and influence of the Molly Maguires on American labor history.

5. "The Amazing Pennsylvania Canals," by William H. Shank, P.E. The American Canal and Transportation Center, 809 Rathton Road, York, PA 17403, 1981, 128 pages softcover, $9.00. An extensive and

scholarly examination of the history, growth and decline of the Pennsylvania canals. Mr. Shank brings an immense knowledge to bear, and he writes in a very engaging manner. Numerous pictures and drawings. A fine introduction to the subject of canals. The drawings on page 29 are from "The Amazing Pennsylvania Canals."

Recommended Listening

"Last Day of the Northern Field," by the Donegal Weavers. Nineteen tunes chronicle the hard life of the miner. Some of them are bright and perky, others are sad, appropriate to the subject matter. These songs are done in a traditional Irish way.

1 Coaltown Road
2 Miners Strawberries
3 Jigs: Market Town,
 Scatter the Mud
4 Dark as a Dungeon
5 Jake & Jack Are Miners
6 Hard Times
7 Last Day of the Northern
 Field
8 Ashley Planes
9 Stigma
10 Ned of the Hill

11 Sugar Notch Entombment
12 Sons of Molly Maguire
13 May God Above/Reel:
 Drover's Lad
14 Old Miner's Refrain
15 Lost Creek
16 When the Breaker Starts
 Up Full Time
17 Canalboat Rattlesnake
18 Old Joe Clark/ Liberty/
 Boil the Cabbage
19 My Sweetheart's the Mule
 in the Mine

The Donegal Weavers are: Joseph P. Jones, John D. Dougherty, Ray Stephens, Emmet Burke, and George Yeager. This tape may be ordered from: The Wyoming Historical and Geological Society, 49 South Franklin Street, Wilkes-Barre, PA, 18701. Please write for current prices.

Acknowledgments

The craft of writing is a lonely one. There are those whose encouragement, inspiration, and kind words have been of the highest value in carrying on the endeavor.

William Ingram	Leo Weiner
Christine Goldbeck	Richard McKeever
John C. Brennan	Tom Johnson (UMW of A)
Patrick Campbell	Alice Wayne
Thomas Barrett	Charles J. Mullen
Genia Miller	Marjorie Bowie
Judge John Lavelle	William H. Shank
John Lindermuth	Robert Fields
Inga Chesney	Carol Baldwin
Robert J. Throckmorton	Wm. Robert Miller
Jack A. Pritchard	Anne Feeney
Tom McBride	Robert L. Birch

Many others have helped, including some who didn't know they were doing it at the time. My appreciation to all.

INDEX

122

Eric McKeever

Eric McKeever was born in Shamokin on January 4, 1930, at 400 West Arch Street. He graduated in 1947 from Shamokin High school and embarked on an extended career with various governmental agencies: the Veterans Administration, United States Post Office, and longest of all, the Baltimore County Department of Health. Now in retirement, he conducts a worldwide pen pal network. He is married, with one son, Edgar, who is in college.

124

The pictures of the mine tipple, peg shanty, air shaft, and mine car were made at the Lackawanna Coal Mine at McDade Park in Scranton, Pennsylvania. This mine is adjacent to the Anthracite Heritage Museum, with tours available to visitors. The mine was an actual working coal mine until 1966. Words are inadequate to convey the feelings aroused by being underground where men toiled throughout their working lives. The museum contains many other machines and tools associated with the early days of industry in Pennsylvania.

All drawings were done by Edgar McKeever of Baltimore. The typesetting and page lay-out were done by DeeDee Hendrickson Leone of TyPerfect Words, Inc. in Bel Air, Maryland. The book printing was done by Victor Graphics, Inc. of Baltimore, Maryland. First printing, 1992, copyright 1992 by Eric McKeever. Additional copies are available from the author. This book will be available on audio tape for the hearing impaired. The book is distributed nationwide by Baker and Taylor. To inquire about prices and shipping contact Eric McKeever, 8506 Valleyfield Road, Lutherville, Maryland 21093, U.S.A.